HOUSING THE ELDERLY

HOUSING THE ELDERLY

Options and Design

Francis and Francesca Weal

Mitchell · London

© Francis and Francesca Weal 1988
First published 1988

All rights reserved. No part of this publication
may be reproduced, in any form or by any means,
without permission from the Publisher.

Typeset by Tameside Filmsetting, Ltd.
Ashton-under-Lyne, Lancashire
and printed in Great Britain by
The Bath Press Ltd
Bath, Somerset
Published by The Mitchell Publishing Company Limited
4 Fitzhardinge Street, London W1H 0AH
A subsidiary of B. T. Batsford Limited

British Library Cataloguing in Publication Data
Weal, Francis
  Housing the elderly: options and design.
  1. Sheltered housing units for old persons.
  Architectural design
  I. Title   II. Weal, Francesca
  728.3′1′043

ISBN 0-7134-5416-4

CONTENTS

FOREWORD 7

PREFACE 9

ACKNOWLEDGEMENTS 11

1 INTRODUCTION: THE EVOLUTION OF HOUSING FOR THE ELDERLY 13

2 CATEGORIES OF SHELTERED HOUSING 18

   Reasons for entering sheltered housing
   Moving on from sheltered housing
   Categories of sheltered housing
   Service provision
   Communal facilities and privacy
   Size
   Typical sheltered housing layouts
      Category 1: the active elderly
      Category 2: warden/housekeeper service
      Category $2\frac{1}{2}$: the frail elderly

3 SITE LOCATION, ENVIRONMENT, AREA, CARS & SERVICES 34

   Site location and environment
      Service and leisure facilities
      Communications
   Site area, car parking and services
      Site area
      Car spaces and garages
      Services

4 DETAILED DESIGN GUIDANCE 41

   Dwellings and space standards
      entrance
      living room
      kitchen
      bedroom
      bathroom
      orientation and aspect
      extra-care units
   Frail elderly schemes
      the bed-sit flat
   Wardens' dwellings
   Common areas
      entrance foyer
      common room or lounge
      luncheon clubs
      communal WCs
      guest room
      warden's office
      laundry
      telephone kiosk
      refuse disposal
      cleaners' storage
      boiler house
      tank room
      electrical switch room
      battery room
   Communal facilities: frail elderly schemes
      corridors and staircases

5 LANDSCAPE 84

   Vehicular and pedestrian approach
   Public and private space
   Residents' communal outdoor space
   Residents' private outdoor space
   Recreation outdoors
   Elements in the landscape
      hard landscape
      lighting
      external signs
      external seating
      the organic landscape

6 MEANS OF ESCAPE, FIRE PRECAUTIONS, SERVICES AND COMMUNICATIONS 92

   Means of escape
   Fire fighting and alarm equipment
   Services
      heating and cooking
      water supply
      lighting
      lifts
      ventilation
   Communications
      emergency alarms
      telephones
      television aerials

7 RETIREMENT OR SHELTERED HOUSING? 99

   Degrees of care to support independence
   Continuing care
   Integrated care
   Responding to a variety of needs

8 CASE STUDIES 101

   Category 1: Sheltered housing at Wye, Kent
   Category 2: Sheltered housing at Harwell, Oxfordshire
   Category 2: Sheltered housing at Faversham, Kent
   Category 2 (Extra-Care): Sheltered housing at Daventry, Northamptonshire
   Category 2½: Abbeyfield housing at Hayes, Middlesex
   Categories 1, 2 and 2½: Old People's home at Almere, Netherlands

APPENDIX A: DESIGN CHECKLIST 137

   The site and layout
   Access and circulation
   Dwellings
   Warden's dwelling
   Communal facilities

APPENDIX B: LIST OF ORGANISATIONS 140

BIBLIOGRAPHY 142

INDEX 144

FOREWORD

For increasing numbers of people, retirement spans a period of thirty years or more. Often starting before the age of 60, some will achieve the age of 90 + still mentally alert and physically independent. But for most, this period of life will be marked by sad events (such as the death of a spouse), by some degree of physical restriction and, for a few, by mental frailty. The threat which some changes may present can be transformed to opportunity for those who have the choice to live in sheltered housing where the home and its immediate environment are designed around the needs of older people. This book is about such opportunities.

Designing housing for elderly people is full of pitfalls for the innocent or the arrogant architect. Labels such as 'like Colditz', 'institutional', 'paternalistic' have been applied to some of the worst products in the past. Yet sensitivity and imagination, combined with a sound grasp of essentials, have helped to produce range and variety in sheltered housing with continuing evolution towards better standards. An example of this is Anchor's own pioneering work in Housing-with-Care which seeks to combine the best of sheltered housing with the facilities and services for care needed by very frail old people.

Ingrid Gehl, the Danish psychologist, has identified in a clear and simple way the needs which should be borne in mind when designing living environments:

1. Physiological needs: sleep, rest, food, drink, hygiene, sex, light, air, sun.
2. Safety needs: general house safety; avoidance of pollution, noise, accidents; traffic safety.
3. Psychological needs: contact, experience, privacy, activity, play, structuring (to be capable of orientation), identification and aesthetics.

Such advice applies with particular force to housing for older people whose needs are less predictable, more highly variable, than those of younger generations.

Francis and Francesca Weal bring to this book more than twenty years of observation and experience, which they have translated into many delightful and successful sheltered housing schemes. Housing associations, local authorities, housebuilders and their architects will all benefit from the clear and wise guidance they provide here. Above all, I hope that future generations of elderly people will have cause to thank Francis and Francesca Weal for their contribution to the fuller enjoyment of old age.

Richard Bettesworth
*Chairman, Housing for the Elderly Group,
National Federation of Housing Associations*

PREFACE

The problem of housing the elderly faces all industrialised nations. In the UK there have been many papers written on the needs of the elderly, and sheltered housing has been developed to help them maintain an independent lifestyle with security and comfort. Internationally the developments in the UK have been acknowledged as being in the forefront of this work. In a conference paper on the subject Donohue and Noam[1] record that 'Great Britain has been recognised as world leader in the development of A.I.L. (Assisted Independent Living) accommodation under the title of "Sheltered Housing"'.

[1] Donohue, W. T. and Noam, E., *Assisted Independent Living in Grouped Housing for Older People: A Report on the Situation in European Countries*, Washington, D.C., International Centre for Social Gerontology, 1976

In the past twenty years sheltered housing in the UK has come of age as the problems associated with an ageing community within a sheltered housing environment have become more apparent. The degree of housing and service needed is debated and the interaction between these parts of the 'sheltered' framework discussed. The distinction varies between independent living for the elderly and care in a nursing home.

Individual organisations have developed their ideas on sheltered housing and provided their architects with design briefs, but to date no comprehensive design guidelines have been published. This book examines current thinking on sheltered housing and offers design guidelines based on unpublished papers and the authors' own experience of designing for the elderly.

Francis and Francesca Weal
London, October 1987

ACKNOWLEDGEMENTS

The authors' experience and knowledge gained in designing for the elderly owes much to the late Tom Stallabrass OBE, founder director of Help the Aged Housing Association UK.

In researching this book the authors acknowledge the help of the Anchor Housing Association in making available research and statistical information; Professor W. R. Keatinge for advice on the effects of cold; Dr R. M. Keatinge for research advice on Chapter 1; the Chapman Bathurst Partnership for guidance on mechanical and electrical services; and architects Phippen Randall & Parkes of the UK, and Herman Hertzberger of the Netherlands, for making available for publication plans and illustrations of their work.

Our thanks are also due to Rosemary Strong for typing the draft, Ann Simon for her assistance in reproducing plans and Sandy Walkington for proof reading.

1. INTRODUCTION: THE EVOLUTION OF HOUSING FOR THE ELDERLY

Sheltered housing is now a familiar solution to the problems of housing the elderly. It combines the security of group living with an environment which should ideally be designed carefully for the physical limitations of ageing. Yet less than ten years ago it was relatively unknown in the UK outside local government and pioneer housing associations. Many members of the general public were unaware of its existence, and statutory bodies did not have any guidelines on the classification of this type of development for implementing their byelaws. Developers, if they were aware of its existence at all, did not see any market potential in it until one much publicised developer who saw the gap in the market and capitalised on it.

What has happened to change this perspective? The answer is that there has been a growing awareness on the part of old people from all walks of life that their current environment is unsatisfactory. It is now evident that sheltered housing can provide an interim solution for growing dependence without the need for admission to nursing homes or geriatric wards which are expensive to run. There is also an awareness of the remarkable potential in encouraging home-owners to realise their equity to finance a more comfortable lifestyle in a smaller home.

In addition elderly people constitute a far larger percentage of the general population than ever before in Europe and the United States: the trend seems likely to continue for the foreseeable future. Table 1 shows the elderly as a percentage of the population of England and Wales. The projections do not depend on fertility projections (notoriously the most inaccurate part of these surveys). The slight dip in the statistics for 65 and over, then 75 and over, for 2001 and 2018 respectively, could be due to the fall-off in birth rate during the Second World War. The figure for 65 and over for 2018 takes in the start of the 'baby boom' – the cut-off being 1953.

Table 1 **The elderly as a percentage of the population in England and Wales**

Population total		65 and over	75 and over
1933[1]	40,350,000	3,120,200 (7.73%)	872,900 (2.16%)
1964[2]	47,511,000	5,715,800 (12.03%)	2,067,700 (4.35%)
1984[3]	49,763,600	7,473,900 (15.02%)	3,167,400 (6.36%)
2001[4]	51,270,000	7,287,000 (14.21%)	3,314,000 (6.46%)
2018[4]	52,550,000	8,006,000 (15.24%)	3,195,000 (6.08%)

[1]*Registrar General's Statistical Review of England and Wales for the year 1933* (New annual series No. 13) Part 1: *Tables. Medical*, HMSO 1934

[2]*Registrar General's Statistical Review of England and Wales for the year 1964*, Part 1: *Tables. Medical*, HMSO 1966

[3]*Mortality Statistics 1984*, Series DH1, no. 16, Office of Population Censuses and Surveys, HMSO 1986

[4]*Population projections 1978–2018*, Series PP2, no. 10, Office of Population Censuses and Surveys, prepared by Government Actuary in consultation with the Registrar General, HMSO 1980

INTRODUCTION: THE EVOLUTION OF HOUSING FOR THE ELDERLY

It is worth considering why the numbers of elderly have increased. A popular misconception is that recent advances in modern medicine, with its elaborate surgical techniques and drug therapy, have caused people to live far longer than they would otherwise have done. In fact, modern medicine has barely increased the limit of life expectancy of *homo sapiens sapiens*.[1] A cursory glance at gravestones will reveal that many of our ancestors achieved a ripe old age of 80 plus and that the life expectancy of a 70-year-old in 1930 is very similar to that of a 70-year-old today. What has changed is that many more can attain these venerable heights.

The death rate in both sexes ages 65–74 was 64 per thousand in 1841–50; in 1961–70 it had reduced to 39 per thousand. A drop of 39% is not dramatic when compared to the results for children. The mortality rate at ages 0–14 in 1841–50 was 66 per thousand compared to 4.73 per thousand in 1961–70: a drop of 93%. Children accounted for slightly less than half the deaths – 47% compared to 2% in 1975.[2]

The responsibility for this change lies in the hands of those individuals who instigated reforms in basic health care and sanitation, and improved standards of housing and nutrition in the nineteenth and early twentieth centuries, thus reducing a large amount of avoidable ill-health and death.

The early nineteenth century was inauspicious for people who wanted to achieve the biblical three-score years and ten. The Agricultural Revolution combined with the employment demands of the Industrial Revolution and accelerated the drift to the cities in search of work. This led to vast numbers of poorly-nourished people being crammed together in extraordinarily high densities, with little or no access to clean water and no sewage disposal facilities. Such a concentration of population and such a ready method of ensuring infection and reinfection meant that tuberculosis, cholera, typhus, dysentery and a host of other malevolent viral and bacterial infections were endemic. This would be sufficient to ensure that most people would not reach old age, but in addition there were unsupervised hazards at work, uncontrolled pollution from factories and widespread adulteration of foodstuffs with substances which make our anxieties over 'E' numbers seem tame by comparison.

The efforts of the reformers of nineteenth century England – the first country in the world to be faced with such a problem on such a scale – were directed towards improving the lot of the poor. They were spurred on by pressure from the rich who were dismayed by the conditions which made cities more dangerous to live in than the countryside. They realised that separating humankind from its effluent would improve matters. The development of the germ theory was documented in 1798 when Edward Jenner made his empirical observations that milkmaids who had had cow-pox did not seem as prone to smallpox as others. Inoculation techniques, using material from the pustules of cows suffering from cow-pox, gave protection, for those who would accept it, from smallpox which had up till then been a terrible scourge of all age-groups.

Hand-in-hand went early byelaws to limit density, admit more sunlight (proof against rickets) and make structures safer to live in. The Public Health Act of 1875 was the precursor of modern building regulations. Statutes were introduced to prevent obviously poisonous substances being introduced into food and doctors inveighed against baby medicines such as 'Doctor Godfrey's Cordial' which was used to quieten babies and contained opium. Antiseptic surgery, which involved spraying everything with carbolic acid (including the surgeon); aseptic surgery – which involved hand washing – cleanliness, and reforms in nursing practice by Florence Nightingale, made hospitals safer places, from which one was more likely to emerge alive.

These advances in environmental health ensured that more babies survived infancy and became healthier adults.

It is not recent 'high-tech' advances in modern medicine, therefore, which have been responsible

[1] Thomas McKeown, *The Role of Medicine*, Nuffield Hospitals Trust, 1976, Chapter 6 and *passim*

[2] *Trends in Mortality 1951–1975*, Series DH1 no. 3, Office of Population Censuses and Surveys, HMSO, 1978

INTRODUCTION: THE EVOLUTION OF HOUSING FOR THE ELDERLY

for the increase in the number of elderly but a long-term establishment of basic principles of health care and an improvement in living conditions. In the last decade, attention to preventive medicine in the US and, latterly, in the UK may mean that the proportion of people we describe as 'elderly' may increase further as a percentage of the population.

Areas of possible improvement include:

1. Decreases in over-nutrition and smoking, the main causes of the 'Western' diseases, heart attacks and strokes, which still cause most of the deaths in people under retirement age.

2. Gentle but sustained exercise giving general fitness, a sense of well-being and prolonged mobility. In addition, some experts believe that it has possible benefits in delaying the onset of osteoporosis, the 'thin bone' syndrome common in elderly women which results in broken bones after even minor falls or knocks.

None of the above will give absolute protection from frailness of mind and body, the most distressing features of old age, but if more are to achieve old age it is important to society and to their own self-respect that they are as healthy and as independent as possible.

Apart from improvements in preventive medicine, other factors at work mean that Western society may be characterised for a few decades by a greater preponderance of elderly as a proportion of the population. The products of the post-war baby boom are now at child-rearing stage, but the birth rate of many Western nations is continuing to diminish. The young are at the greatest risk from AIDS but as yet it is too early to say what effect this disease will have on the population profile.

Our society has a tradition of attempting to meet the housing needs of the elderly. The almshouse movement dates back to the twelfth century, when accommodation for the sick and needy was built at the gates of the monasteries. These 'hospitals' were charitable foundations, wealthy people providing in their wills for the building and the care of the occupants, and many of the resulting dwellings are of great architectural merit. The concept survived the Reformation and in England is still active. Many towns still possess little terraces or courtyards of miniaturised dwellings whose architecture often makes reference to its monastic antecedents. As a result of the later growth of a town they are often very close to the town centre. They are still popular although the design of the older dwellings does not make concessions to the frailties of old age. The clustering of them induces a feeling of security, while location near the centre of town, together with physical attractiveness, make this type of dwelling a valid choice for the hale elderly. These days the state pension provides basic financial assistance and the almshouse occupants, chosen on grounds of need, pay a small rental towards the upkeep of the properties.

The almshouse concept is not confined to England. Examples in Europe include those found in the Netherlands and Germany.[3]

In the Netherlands 'hofjes' or 'small courts' can be found. These consist of small houses built around a pleasant court, single-aspected, with one room on the ground floor and one room upstairs. They also were charitable foundations and often named after the founder. Like the English almshouses, some are still used for housing the elderly and have been suitably upgraded with proper sanitary facilities. Their defensive, introverted arrangement, 'fortified' by monumental entrance gateways, gives a sense of security to the inhabitants. An early German initiative is Die Fuggerei in Augsburg. James Fugger the Rich and his brothers established one of the oldest welfare settlements in Europe through a deed of foundation in 1521. It is a self-contained settlement intended for 'undeservedly impoverished Catholic citizens of Augsburg'. It has its own shops and a church. No single people are admitted – although widows' quarters are provided – and the head of the household must be at least 55 years old. Single children can stay with their parents. It is still used.

---

[3]Information from Beyer and Nierstraz, *Housing the Aged in Western Countries*, Elsevier, Amsterdam, 1967

INTRODUCTION: THE EVOLUTION OF HOUSING FOR THE ELDERLY

Unfortunately, those in almshouses were the lucky ones. The workhouse was a threat to all poor elderly up to the turn of the century; many couples ended up there on becoming too old to earn a living. The workhouse had separate entrances and living quarters for men and women, and the cruellest blow to many an old couple was separation from each other. The music hall song 'My Old Dutch', telling of a forty-year attachment which 'don't seem a day too much', was often sung in front of a painted backdrop depicting the two entrances of the workhouse; a poignant touch for those who remembered its significance.

The philanthropic movement in the nineteenth century laid the foundations for modern local authority housing and, more particularly, for the growth of the housing association movement. Both these bodies house more elderly than the private sector and have a great deal of experience in this field.

The growth in the number of elderly in our population means that our response to housing the elderly should no longer be considered as a public sector obligation to the poorer sections of the community. There are underlying social trends that make specialised housing for the elderly an attractive option for a wide range of income groups.

In the UK, before the Second World War, oral tradition has it that an elderly person was looked after by the family or, failing that, by other members of the close-knit urban community – which by now had become established and stable. In the homes of the better-off, empty rooms created by the reduction in servants meant that space could be found for an elderly relative. In fact, the percentage of old people in institutions is now lower than in 1900 and more are looked after at home. Nevertheless, the current high level of home ownership has led to a society in which property is bought and sold according to size of family and proximity to preferred schooling and jobs. We are expected to be mobile and to behave accordingly.

Nowadays, members of the family may find themselves far from each other yet not necessarily experiencing a diminution in family loyalty. At first, this is not a problem as the telephone remains a constant source of contact. However, problems begin when the elderly become too frail to look after their own home satisfactorily – a situation which gets worse on the death of a partner. The sex roles are more rigidly defined among the older generation and old men in particular find it difficult to cope, lacking skill in cooking, cleaning and mending. Old women likewise may need someone to carry out the home maintenance tasks that their husbands might have undertaken when alive. At this age, too, old friends are dying and support networks begin to crumble, while children are far away. The distant child may wish to help but it is often not practical for the younger family to relocate. 'Mother' or 'Father' has become a problem. This is when sheltered housing is seen as a solution by the family.

It is a sad fact that many elderly people are frightened by their environment. Although nineteenth-century inner cities could be almost lawless – certain parts of London's East End, for example, being no-go areas for the police – the period between the two world wars was remarkable for its low crime rate. Many elderly who were young adults at that time are quite dismayed by what they perceive to be a slide into lawlessness. In fact, although television, radio and newspapers graphically bring isolated incidents of sickening violence to the forefront, young men are far more likely to be attacked in inner-city areas than any other group. But the perception of a violent society imprisons many elderly in their homes. Many see sheltered housing as a remedy for this, though they may not admit this as a major motivation for their move.

Among the better-off, a major factor encouraging the move to 'retirement housing' (as it is called by private developers) is the attraction of releasing capital tied up in a now-too-large house, in order to allow a more comfortable lifestyle in a secure home, surrounded by like-minded individuals and with building maintenance problems taken care of by the management of the scheme. The scheme

INTRODUCTION: THE EVOLUTION OF HOUSING FOR THE ELDERLY

becomes like a club. Studies in the US have revealed that the 'active elderly' – the 55 plus age group – are at the pinnacle of their spending power. They have left behind the financial obligations imposed by babies/children/students and are at the peak of their careers. This class of elderly people has been called 'the empty nesters'. At this time of life, they are taking stock of their position and are susceptible to attempts to help them capitalise on the equity locked up in their family home. This age group and income bracket is now perceived as a huge growth market by UK developers, whose US counterparts are already well down the trail.

Sheltered housing (or retirement housing), is the response by our society to a growing need. No longer perceived as the province of charity alone, it is regarded as a positive benefit to be exploited by all income groups. Sheltered housing is a convenient term describing specialised housing for the elderly, but it has become wide in its application. This is because it is impossible to class the elderly as a discrete group with discrete needs. They represent a cross-section of society with a variety of incomes – and of degrees of dependency.

The stages of life can be listed as:

Birth
Decreasing dependency
Adulthood
Increasing dependency
Death

Our concern is with the area of increasing dependency. It is now clear that there are important gradations of this. Many old people can live quite happily, given minimal support – but without this minimal support a higher-dependency type of care needs to be provided, with the attendant costs to society. Sheltered housing is the architectural response to this category of increasing dependency. However, as will be shown in the ensuing chapters, the definition of sheltered housing is subject to further divisions and to subtle shifts in design parameters.

2 | CATEGORIES OF SHELTERED HOUSING

In the USA the title of 'warden' is associated with penal authority, but in the UK it has a different connotation, suggesting care and service.

In the organisation of a sheltered housing complex there must be someone responsible to the residents for day-to-day problems. The degree of responsibility undertaken will vary from one organisation to another, according to the range of service on offer to the residents. The most basic service is the provision of management to take care of the estate, the fabric of the building, common services, lighting, etc. This service can be supplied by a non-resident manager. At the other end of the service scale are resident staff on hand to deal with emergencies. In the UK this residential management role is assigned to a 'warden' or 'housekeeper'. Throughout this book we have used the UK term 'warden' as it implies not only the general duties of a 'housekeeper' but also the provision of a friendly but unobtrusive service giving assistance in emergency.

Before discussing the wide variety of housing categories for the elderly, it is worth considering that the client group includes some remarkable people, including the Queen Mother, Ronald Reagan, Freya Stark and Sister Teresa – a very select list but worth remembering to avoid patronising those for whom we design.

There is a wide variety of housing concepts for the elderly, ranging from development with minimal services – generally known as Proximate or Category 1 housing – to maximum services which are found in Congregate or Category $2\frac{1}{2}$ housing. Beyond Category $2\frac{1}{2}$, that is very sheltered or frail elderly housing, we leave the realm of independent living for that of care in residential homes where the daily life of residents depends on nursing skills, a subject outside the scope of our study. This chapter explores and illustrates these different categories of independent or semi-independent housing. We will also consider why people opt to move into sheltered accommodation. In the commercial sector, housing for the elderly is marketed generally as 'retirement homes'. In the public sector, which includes housing associations, most of the dwellings are rented on a subsidised basis. Some housing associations have developed equity-sharing schemes, with dwellings sold on a leasehold basis.

Since the late sixties the development of sheltered housing by housing associations and local authorities has boomed, although in recent years this development has tailed off under government financial restraints. By the late seventies, as public sheltered housing had won a reputation for user satisfaction, commercial development with units for sale began to attract private finance. Today there is a ready market for sheltered or retirement housing at all socio-economic levels. Retirement housing is a specialised market calling for informed judgements on user motivation and an appreciation of residents' needs. Before looking at options in design it is worthwhile considering why people move into this specialised environment in the first place.

Reasons for entering sheltered housing

Insights into motivation for the move into public sheltered housing can be obtained from a research survey carried out on behalf of the Anchor Housing Association.[1] This survey, commissioned by the Association, is of value as the sample was based on the largest stock of sheltered housing in the control of any one organisation, with tenants distributed throughout the UK. Whilst caution is needed in assigning the elderly to socio-economic groups, it is clear that the survey covers unskilled to junior management groups. The survey provides a profile of typical tenants as follows:

> . . . a widowed woman in her mid-to-late seventies with generally one or two surviving children who are typically middle-aged (between 40 and 60). Nearly a fifth of the tenants are still married; those who are widowed divide fairly equally between those who have recently been widowed and those who have been widowed for a substantial proportion of their lives.

Anchor Housing Association tenants are selected principally from people in housing need, that is, from poor or unsuitable accommodation, remote from shopping facilities and having a low income. The survey identified certain key reasons why this group of elderly people opted to move out of their existing homes.

Examined under three headings are 1,550 reasons given by 863 tenants:

1. *Health/Bereavement*
Anxieties about the respondent's or spouse's health was an important factor. Deteriorating health or periods of illness raise problems for isolated elderly people when there is no one on hand to offer help. Bereavement following the death of the spouse or cohabitant can lead to loneliness, depression and a lack of security. Of 446 reasons associated with health and bereavement, 312 were health-related.

[1] Fennell, G., *Anchor Tenants' Survey*, Anchor Housing Association/University of East Anglia, 1985

2. *Relatives/Friends*
Positive family reasons figured high in this area. Typically the respondent wished to be nearer to a son, daughter or other relative.

3. *Previous home*
The maintenance and difficulties of coping with the previous home rated high in the list of reasons for moving. Almost half the reasons were related to difficulties in maintaining the house and its garden, or coping with stairs and steps. A significant worry was fear of burglaries and vandalism resulting from a poor environment. Many referred to problems, either of distance or hilly terrain, associated with walking to shops and transport.

The motivation to move for elderly people is varied but there is strong evidence that the key factors are anxiety about declining health and isolation, a wish to be nearer to relatives, and concern at coping with an existing home which is no longer secure and easily run.

With different nuances, it is reasonable to believe that research into higher socio-economic groups would reveal similar reasons for wishing to move out of their homes.

So much for reasons for leaving the old family home. But why move into sheltered housing?

The Anchor survey, having considered the 'push' factor, the motivation for leaving the old home, sought reasons for entering sheltered accommodation – the 'pull' factor.

When respondents were asked to list the importance of various factors underlying their decision to apply for sheltered accommodation the following order of priority emerged:

1. Always warm with central heating
2. No worries about repairs/maintenance of house and garden
3. Nearness to a relative
4. Having a warden on hand
5. No steps or stairs
6. Worries about health
7. Nearness of old home and friends
8. Neighbours of similar age
9. A common room for social activities

CATEGORIES OF SHELTERED HOUSING

Most Anchor tenants come from inadequate housing where the heating is likely to be poor; in Anchor housing tenants do not pay a separate heating bill. The policy of the Association is to ensure that tenants do not 'economise' on heating, so its cost is included in their rent.

People entering sheltered housing from higher income groups will not be motivated in the same way. Used to a good standard of housing, they will expect good heating and amenities. The removal of anxieties about repairs/maintenance of house and garden remains high on the list, however. With retirement, many will want to travel abroad safe in the knowledge that their home is under the watchful eye of a warden/housekeeper/secretary or close neighbour, and that the garden is being maintained.

Higher income groups, accustomed to organising their estate and probably carrying medical insurance, are less attracted by the notion of a 'warden' keeping a friendly eye on them. However, they like the benefit of passing on the day-to-day responsibility for managing the congregate estate to a responsible person. In some schemes this person is known as the 'housekeeper' or 'secretary'. Whatever the euphemism the duties are synonymous with those of the conventional 'warden'.

Successful sheltered housing enhances the quality of life for the resident and provides an unobtrusive aid to independent living. It is not an alternative form of housing. Elderly people occupying houses larger than they need do not see the transition into sheltered housing as trading down but as redistributing resources to allow for an improved lifestyle. Such 'empty nesters' wish to enjoy travel and other social activities now that their children have left home.

Moving on from sheltered housing

Having outlined the motivation for entry into sheltered housing, consideration must be given to the inevitable exit. Studies[2] of population movement into residential care, of people unable to lead an independent life, show that 1% of the UK national sheltered housing population and 0.5% of all elderly moved on into residential care. A pilot study[3] by the Anchor Association reports a higher percentage: 2.4% of Anchor tenants. The Anchor sample includes a higher than average age group, including many aged 80+. This age structure is a legacy of the earlier development of sheltered housing, with rapid growth followed by a slowdown. The pattern has significant implications for developers. In the early days of development with a young-elderly population the support services will not be under pressure, but as residents age the care required will become more intensive.

The disabilities of the young-elderly, and in this group we encompass the age group 65–74, are not significantly different from those of the age group 55–64. However, the 75 + group are significantly more susceptible to fatal falls as their mobility is impaired.

The policy for the future care of residents must be firmly established at the design stage, and decisions made on what resources are to be made available for supporting them in their declining years. This introduces the idea of service: will the development be basic accommodation designed to mobility standards suitable only for the active elderly or will it be 'service rich' to cater for all eventualities? If only basic accommodation is planned, some hard decisions must be made at the outset regarding residents' right of tenure if and when they can no longer cope.

The size and service content of sheltered housing schemes varies considerably, from small groups of bungalows to large complexes incorporating shops and nursing facilities. Generally schemes in the UK favour groups of 25 to 35 flats served by a warden. In the USA whole townships of

[2]Butler, A., *Sheltered Housing for the Elderly*, Leeds University, 1984

[3]Way, A. and Fennell, G., *Anchor Tenants moving from Sheltered Housing into Residential Care*, University of East Anglia, 1985

congregate and proximate living for the elderly have been developed, such as Sun City, Arizona; whilst in Holland schemes at Amsterdam and Almere-Haven provide environments for the active elderly on a scale not attempted in the UK.

Categories of sheltered housing

For convenience some categorisation is necessary in order to explore different patterns of development. Sheltered housing categories and standards in the UK originated with Government Circular 82/69.[4] This circular introduced the idea of two categories of accommodation for the elderly, with mandatory minimum space standards for schemes in the public sector. It also promulgated higher standards of heating, safety measures and additional aids for old people. The two categories were defined as:

1. Self-contained Dwellings (Category 1)
2. Grouped Flatlets with warden's supervision (Category 2)

The Category 1 schemes envisaged groups of bungalows or flats without a warden. A common room, guest room and emergency alarm system were considered as optional extras attracting extra funding if provided.

Category 2 schemes of grouped flatlets were deemed to include a warden's dwelling with an emergency alarm system connecting each dwelling with the warden's residence. In this category, a common room with a tea kitchen and WC, laundry room and telephone were included as mandatory requirements.

The main thrust of the circular was to define standards of space and design enabling the elderly to maintain an independent way of life, in an environment planned for sociability where they could avoid loneliness and isolation.

Curiously, 'mobility' standards (which include such provisions as doorways wide enough for a wheelchair, and ramped access) were not insisted upon.

A decade after implementation of the Category 1 and 2 schemes, the problems associated with an ageing community began to emerge. Ageing residents tended to become less healthy and more frail, and to be more frequently confined to bed. Illnesses became severe and chronic, causing acute problems for the managers of the schemes and the other inhabitants. Short of sending residents to a nursing home, where the institutional environment sapped their confidence, little could be done to help given the limitations of the resources provided in the schemes.

The residential nursing home, or Part 3 accommodation, to which they might be referred, is a totally different environment and quite unsuitable for most elderly people suffering a temporary disability. There is very little privacy, and as a result of being remote from their homes, many surrender their independence and lose the capacity to be rehabilitated. To meet this contingency some Category 2 schemes now include an extra-care unit, a small flatlet for use by a sick resident. Meals and medical requirements are brought in until the patient can return to his or her own flat. A further development has been the provision of frail elderly schemes, a stage between Category 2 accommodation and Part 3 residential nursing homes. These frail elderly schemes we refer to as Category $2\frac{1}{2}$, a mid-way stage between a fully independent lifestyle and a residential nursing home.

The distinction between categories becomes blurred when an overall view of housing needs is applied to a community of people who will progressively deteriorate physically, and where levels of support will have to be increased by the provision of more on-site or peripatetic services.

Heumann and Boldy,[5] in considering variations in sheltered housing types, note three key variables:

---

[4]Ministry of Housing and Local Government, Circular 82/69, 'Housing Standards and Costs: Accommodation specially Designed for Old People', HMSO, 1969

[5]Heumann, L. and Boldy, D., *Housing for the Elderly*, Croom Helm, 1982

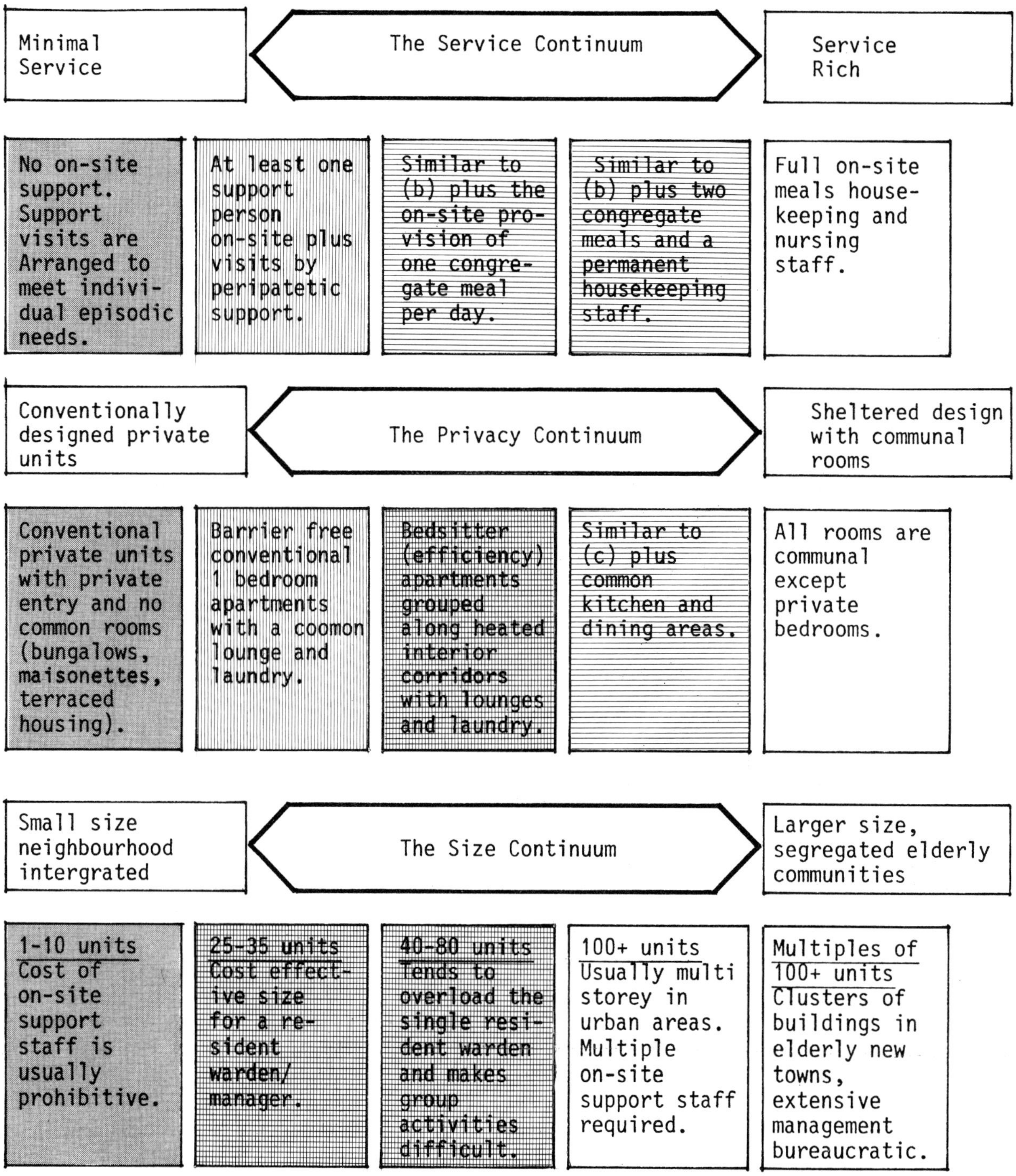

CATEGORIES OF SHELTERED HOUSING

Minimal Service	The Service Continuum	Service Rich

No on-site support. Support visits are Arranged to meet individual episodic needs.	At least one support person on-site plus visits by peripatetic support.	Similar to (b) plus the on-site provision of one congregate meal per day.	Similar to (b) plus two congregate meals and a permanent housekeeping staff.	Full on-site meals housekeeping and nursing staff.

Conventionally designed private units	The Privacy Continuum	Sheltered design with communal rooms

Conventional private units with private entry and no common rooms (bungalows, maisonettes, terraced housing).	Barrier free conventional 1 bedroom apartments with a common lounge and laundry.	Bedsitter (efficiency) apartments grouped along heated interior corridors with lounges and laundry.	Similar to (c) plus common kitchen and dining areas.	All rooms are communal except private bedrooms.

Small size neighbourhood intergrated	The Size Continuum	Larger size, segregated elderly communities

1-10 units Cost of on-site support staff is usually prohibitive.	25-35 units Cost effective size for a resident warden/manager.	40-80 units Tends to overload the single resident warden and makes group activities difficult.	100+ units Usually multi storey in urban areas. Multiple on-site support staff required.	Multiples of 100+ units Clusters of buildings in elderly new towns, extensive management bureaucratic.

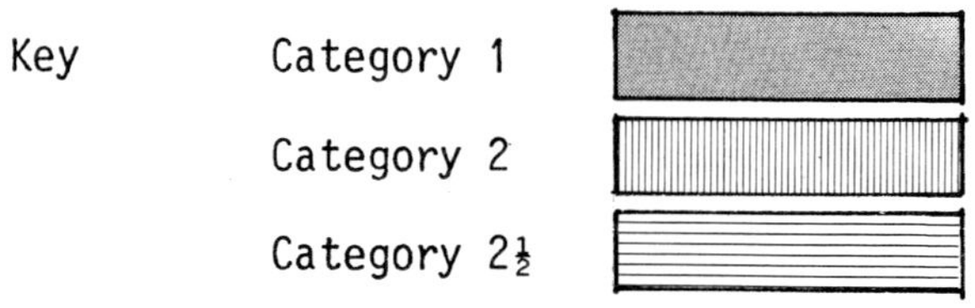

Key
Category 1
Category 2
Category 2½

Fig. 1   Characteristics of different categories of housing applied to Heumann and Boldy's continuum scale of variations in sheltered housing

1. The way in which services are provided
2. The extent of private or communal living arrangements
3. The overall size of the scheme

Applying these variables on a scale continuum they provide a useful matrix of variations in sheltered housing types. (See Figure 1.)

We will now consider the impact that these variables have on the design of a scheme.

Service Provision

Minimum service (Category 1)

Where no provision is made for on-site support the 'sheltered' element of the scheme will be supplied by mutual self-help. A community will be created where privacy is respected, but where through skilful layout residents can keep an eye on the comings and goings of neighbours. The courtyard layout with separate entries to dwellings is an example of this, where the dwellings have a public face looking on to the courtyard, and a private side for sitting outdoors. Central to the design of any sheltered scheme is provision for mobility. Doorways must be wide enough, and rooms and equipment designed to facilitate easy movement for the resident who may temporarily or permanently require personal movement aids such as a walking stick, frame or wheelchair. Steps must be avoided and access to dwellings should be ramped. Where bedrooms or bathrooms are situated on an upper floor, the stair access should be generous in size to permit the installation of a stair lift at a later stage if required. In the design of flats, where lifts are not incorporated, private entrance and stair access to upper floor dwellings should be avoided. It is advisable to provide a grouped entrance and stair access, where, in the event of a resident falling on the stairs, his or her plight will be discovered soon by other residents. Provision should be made for an alarm call system to alert outside agencies, family, friends, or designated support groups, in the event of a fall or other emergency.

Housekeeper/warden service (Category 2)

The conventional scheme includes the service of a housekeeper or warden. Usually this person is resident in the scheme. However, some developments have been promoted with the housekeeper living off-site, in an attempt to decrease the stress that can arise for the warden or housekeeper where residents may have come to expect a 24-hour service. The role and duties attached to the post must be determined early on. Minimum duties would include acting as the contact for emergency calls and liaising with the scheme management board; additional support services, such as medical and chiropodic, would be called on when required.

Provision of meals (Category $2\frac{1}{2}$)

Service provision in warden-supported schemes may be enriched by the provision of one meal a day.

As we have seen, a gap has been identified between the on-site service found in standard sheltered housing schemes (Category 2) and the full service provision provided in a Residential Nursing Home (Part 3 Accommodation). Residents in a Category 2 scheme may temporarily suffer a disability that cannot be coped with by the services provided, but a move into residential nursing care may be inappropriate. The response to this problem has been the development of very sheltered housing or frail elderly schemes (Category $2\frac{1}{2}$). The service provision in such schemes includes dining facilities. These can range from the simple preparation of one cooked meal a day to full restaurant facilities. With the enrichment of service facilities provision must be made for additional housekeeping staff, working in shifts to cover the additional work.

Full On-Site Services: Residential Nursing Homes (Part Three Accommodation)

The residential nursing home is a specialised provision for the elderly where the residents must by definition surrender their self-reliance. The design of these institutions does not fall within the scope of this book. Some sheltered housing schemes have been built with a nursing home included as an extension of normal sheltered housing accommodation. Private developments of this type are taking place in the UK, but not all authorities feel that they are either necessary or desirable. Retirement Security Ltd, a company providing retirement homes and headed by Robert Bessel, who has considerable experience of housing the elderly, takes the view that with the exception of aggressive psychosis, normal senility can be coped with within the framework of a Category $2\frac{1}{2}$ or frail elderly scheme. Meals can be provided and nursing staff brought in to care for residents within their own homes, a more caring concept than the institutional framework which causes many residents to lose all independence.

Communal Facilities and Privacy

Conventional Units (Category 1)
These usually take the form of houses or flats with provision for mobility and for emergency calls. Communal facilities such as common rooms and laundries need not be provided. Privacy and independence are characteristic of such developments.

Conventional Flats (Category 2)
Privacy and self-reliance are still respected in such a scheme but additional background support is introduced and greater provision is made for social interchange. The warden or housekeeper's duties can vary from just being there in case of emergency to daily ringing around on an intercom to see if all is well. Common rooms for social and utility use are standard provisions. The smallest schemes are provided with a common lounge, a laundry and a guest room facility. Larger schemes may include space for hobbies, hairdressing rooms and separate lounges.

Very Sheltered (or Frail Elderly) Housing (Category $2\frac{1}{2}$)
These developments, with their extra services on site, require additional rooms for the preparation of meals and dining, provision for assisted bathrooms, extra-care flats for temporary use, additional accommodation for a deputy warden and extra staff provision. Very sheltered schemes should be considered as aids to independent living and not institutions. Wherever possible the residents should be encouraged to care for themselves, the extra services on site being there in a support role. Where residents need support there is a corresponding loss of privacy, but the idea is to return the resident to independence as soon as health and physical factors permit.

Residential Nursing Home (Part 3 Accommodation)
This has a very high service content with nursing as the prime function, but there is little privacy apart from private bedrooms.

Size

Category 1
Generally these developments are most successful in small groups of up to 20 units where they can be integrated into the local community without creating a ghetto. However, in urban situations larger schemes may succeed.

Category 2
In the provision of warden and communal facilities, the size of development is determined by economics and resources. The most cost-effective size, where a resident warden is to be employed, is 25 to 35 units. Additional units will overburden the warden unless provision is made for a deputy warden. In schemes of 35 to 70 units two resident wardens would be required, working in shifts.

Consideration must be given to wardens' holidays and time off. In small schemes a deputy warden may be employed to cover holidays, using the guest accommodation to live in.

Category $2\frac{1}{2}$
The commitment of schemes for the frail elderly to 24-hour coverage requires careful consideration of how such schemes will be managed. Will they have on-site management with dwellings for

---

Fig. 2   *Category 1: Small group of mutual support dwellings – note visual control of public space*

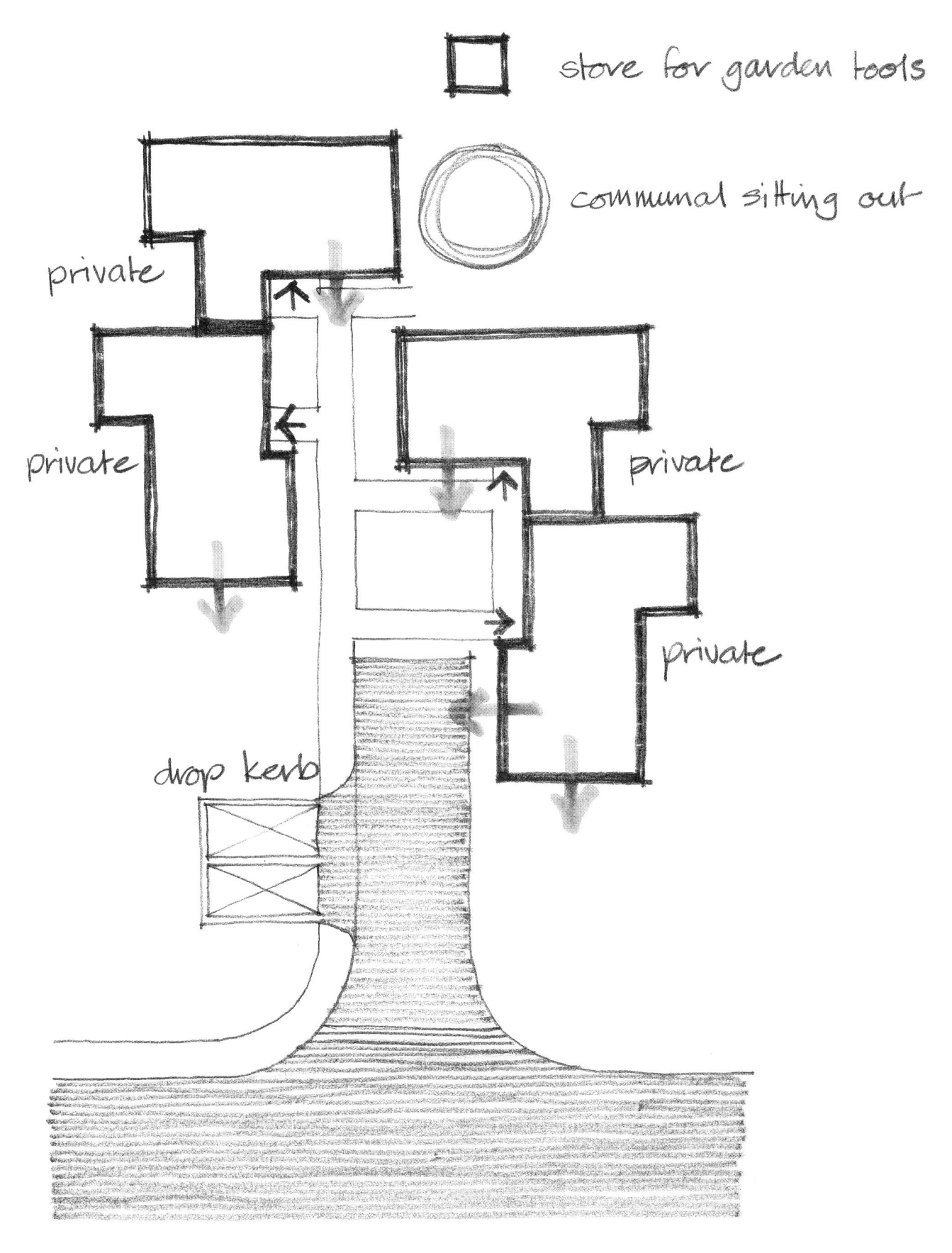

CATEGORIES OF SHELTERED HOUSING

store for garden tools

communal sitting out

private

private

private

private

drop kerb

CATEGORIES OF SHELTERED HOUSING

managers or housekeepers working shifts, or will the management staff live off-site, with work patterns organised by a control office on the scheme? The resources available must match the number of residents. Conventional wisdom is that schemes of approximately 40 dwellings are the most viable.

Typical sheltered housing layouts

Category 1: the active elderly

As we have seen, most Category 1 schemes designed for the active elderly provide little on-site service, maximise privacy and assume a high degree of self-help. In most respects this category of housing is comparable with normal residential design except in specific respects which, if incorporated in all residential design, would overcome difficulties experienced by many house owners. The specific requirements are that provision must be made for mobility, e.g. ramped access to external doors, 900 mm (36 in) door sets, easy access to bathrooms. Being in a self-support group the layout of dwellings should respect privacy but enable residents to keep a discreet eye on comings and goings, with the public side of the scheme designed as 'defensible space'. Figure 2 illustrates these principles for a small group of dwellings. The layout provides for an informally controlled environment, with residents able to monitor visitors by viewing the access points. The choice is available of either sitting out with privacy or meeting neighbours in a communal outdoor area. The keynote of these separate entry self-support groups is the independence enjoyed by the residents. The congregate nature of the development, pooling resources to maintain the external fabric of the buildings and landscape, off-loads the problems onto a management group. The 'defensible space' concept provides security against vandalism and burglaries.

It is advisable to provide two bedrooms to each dwelling in this category of development. The second bedroom may be for guest accommodation, but not infrequently the residents may be a retired couple who are not married or a retired man and wife with a dependant to care for.

Car parking provision will be determined by the location of the site. In central urban sites it may be limited but in rural areas, where the residents are used to car ownership, and for higher socio-economic groups, more car parking spaces may be required. This will be discussed at greater length in Chapter 3.

Category 2: warden/housekeeper service

The level of service support, degree of privacy and scale of development can vary considerably in this category. The basic provision of a warden, with alarm call facilities and full mobility design standards, provides a degree of 'shelter' which enables residents to live independently with security. The inter-relationship of the accommodation provided in this category is illustrated in Figure 3.

The component parts are as follows:

1. Entrance foyer
2. Office
3. Common room and ancillary kitchen and WC
4. Service complex: Lift
    Refuse room
    Boiler room and ancillary plant
5. Laundry
6. Telephone kiosk
7. Guest room
8. Warden's accommodation
9. Residents' flats

The schematic layout incorporates the following principles of design which are common to all Category 2 flat developments:

1. Easily identified residents' access with a private access for the warden.
2. Security and a discreet view of comings and goings provided by the aspect of the office and of the warden's accommodation, with views over the car park and entrance.

CATEGORIES OF SHELTERED HOUSING

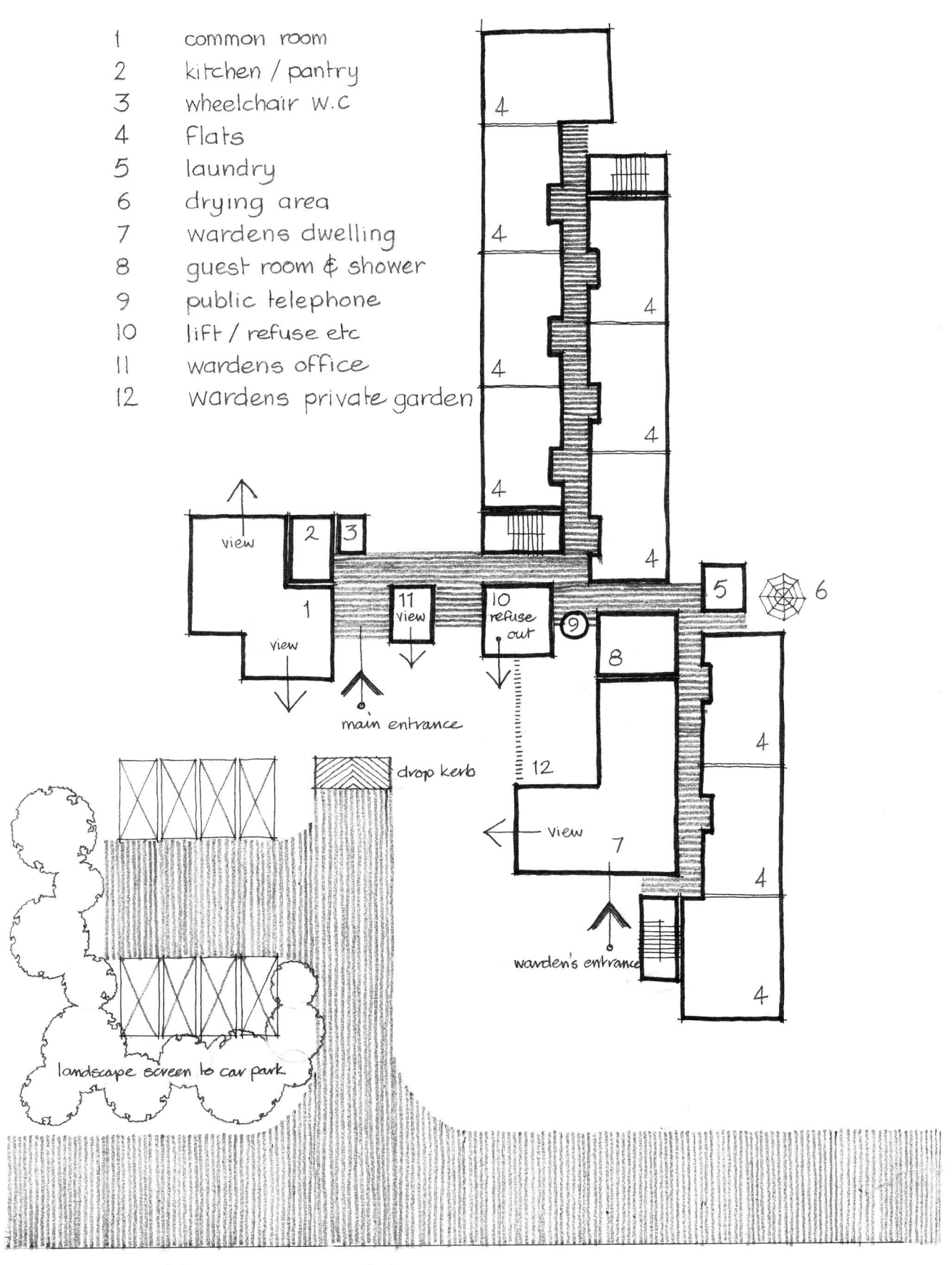

1 common room
2 kitchen / pantry
3 wheelchair W.C
4 flats
5 laundry
6 drying area
7 wardens dwelling
8 guest room & shower
9 public telephone
10 lift / refuse etc
11 wardens office
12 wardens private garden

Fig. 3   *Typical Category 2 accommodation*

CATEGORIES OF SHELTERED HOUSING

3. A common room with views of the car park and onto a private sitting-out space, and a change of view into the scheme. This open aspect with varied views is beneficial to residents, enabling them to enjoy different views to those obtained from their flats. Ancillary to the common room is a small kitchen for light refreshments, and a WC.
4. The service complex. The lift and its machine room, service intakes, central refuse store and boiler room, conveniently positioned and physically isolated from dwellings to prevent noise being transmitted by the structure of the building. The access for refuse collection is sited away from the main entrance.
5. Communal laundry. This is sited away from the route to the common room and, as with the service complex, is physically isolated from dwellings to overcome noise transmission.
6. Telephone kiosk. Situated away from the common room. While required in public housing, a telephone kiosk would not be necessary in a private development.
7. Guest room. The guest room complex incorporates a shower room for communal use. Aspect and orientation are not critical for this room and it may be planned on an upper floor. This room may also be used by a relief warden.
8. Warden's accommodation. It is desirable to plan this as an integral part of the scheme but far enough away from main internal routes to allow some privacy for the warden's family. A separate external access, with private outdoor sitting space, should also be provided where possible. For the warden to be able to keep an eye on residents and visitors a window, preferably in the kitchen or living room, should give a view on to the entrance and car park.
9. Residents' flats. The detailed design of residents' flats is discussed later. There are some principles, however, related to access and the route through the scheme, that should be considered in the overall design of a scheme. It is important that entrance doorways be inviting, and the position of the doorway in relation to route forms a major part of the overall planning considerations. Entrance doorways to flats should not be immediately opposite another flat entrance; the residents' feeling of privacy will be enhanced if doorways are staggered. Double-banked flats, that is flats on either side of a corridor, have been suggested, as in practice this is the most economical layout. Where single-banked flats are economically feasible the problems of natural lighting and proximity of neighbours' doors opposite does not occur. Natural light to corridor access in double-banked layouts can only be achieved at ends of corridors or by designing a break in the run of flats to incorporate a small informal meeting space with external windows. Dead-end corridors without natural light should be avoided.

Windows at ends of corridors can create problems where the wall surface of the corridor has any reflective value. The light shining down the corridor, reflecting down the corridor wall, will highlight the slightest imperfection in the wall surface. Where windows at ends of corridors cannot be avoided, it is good practice to use non-reflective wall and floor surfaces, such as facing bricks and paviors for the 'dead-end' of the corridor. These dead-ends can become a frame for pot plants and help to 'green' the corridor. The best solution for the ends of corridors is to turn the corner to a window. This gives the pleasing effect of a flood of light without the source being immediately obvious. It also invites further exploration and discovery. The routes through the building should be pleasing and inviting with changes of direction lit naturally. Long straight corridors, double-banked, without natural light, are depressing and institutional.

Extra-care units

As previously discussed, a recurring problem for the elderly is periods of ill-health when they are unable to care for themselves. One solution, within the framework of a Category 2 scheme, is to provide an extra-care unit for short-term use followed by rehabilitation in the resident's own flat (see Figure 4). During the period of extra care the resident can enjoy visits from neighbours and friends and not feel isolated from normal life, secure in the knowledge that their flat is close at

CATEGORIES OF SHELTERED HOUSING

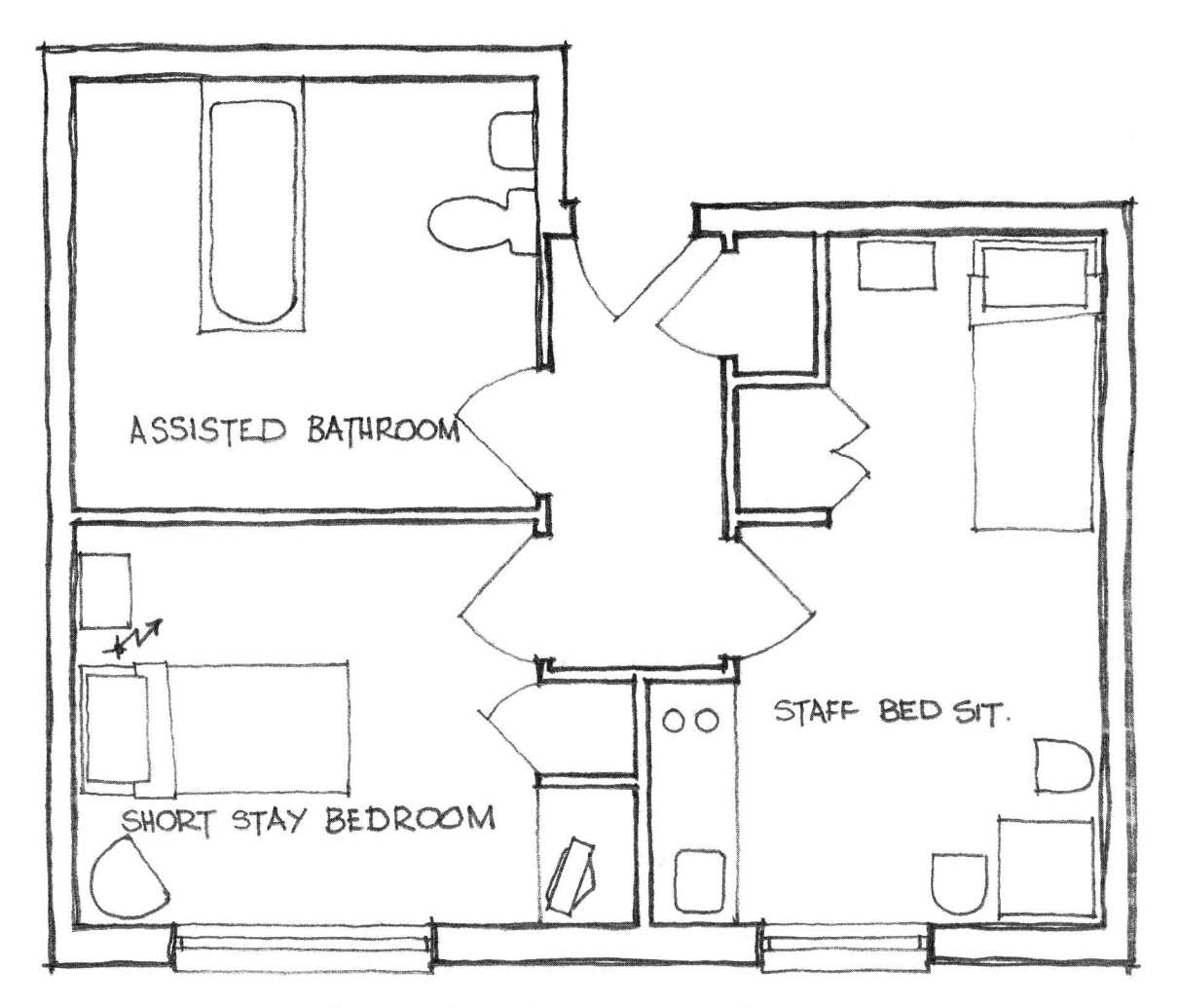

[Floor plan showing: ASSISTED BATHROOM, SHORT STAY BEDROOM, STAFF BED SIT.]

Note: the short stay bedroom should enjoy good and interesting views, the window cill must be low. The staff bed-sit flat should be equiped with a mini-kitchen and a lockable cupboard.

Fig. 4   Typical extra-care unit

hand for them to return to. The provision of an extra-care unit within the framework of a Category 2 scheme enriches the service provision. In practice this provision can only be made in larger schemes where two wardens are on site and the 24-hour cover can be shared.

Category 2½: Frail Elderly Schemes

The design of sheltered housing for the active elderly is now well established. However, 'frail elderly' or 'very sheltered housing' schemes, such as those pioneered by Warwickshire County Council, Abbeyfield and James Butcher Housing Associations, are beginning to receive greater attention as necessary interest in this area of housing/service develops. The cost of running residential care homes and the lack of provision for the frail elderly is focusing attention on

CATEGORIES OF SHELTERED HOUSING

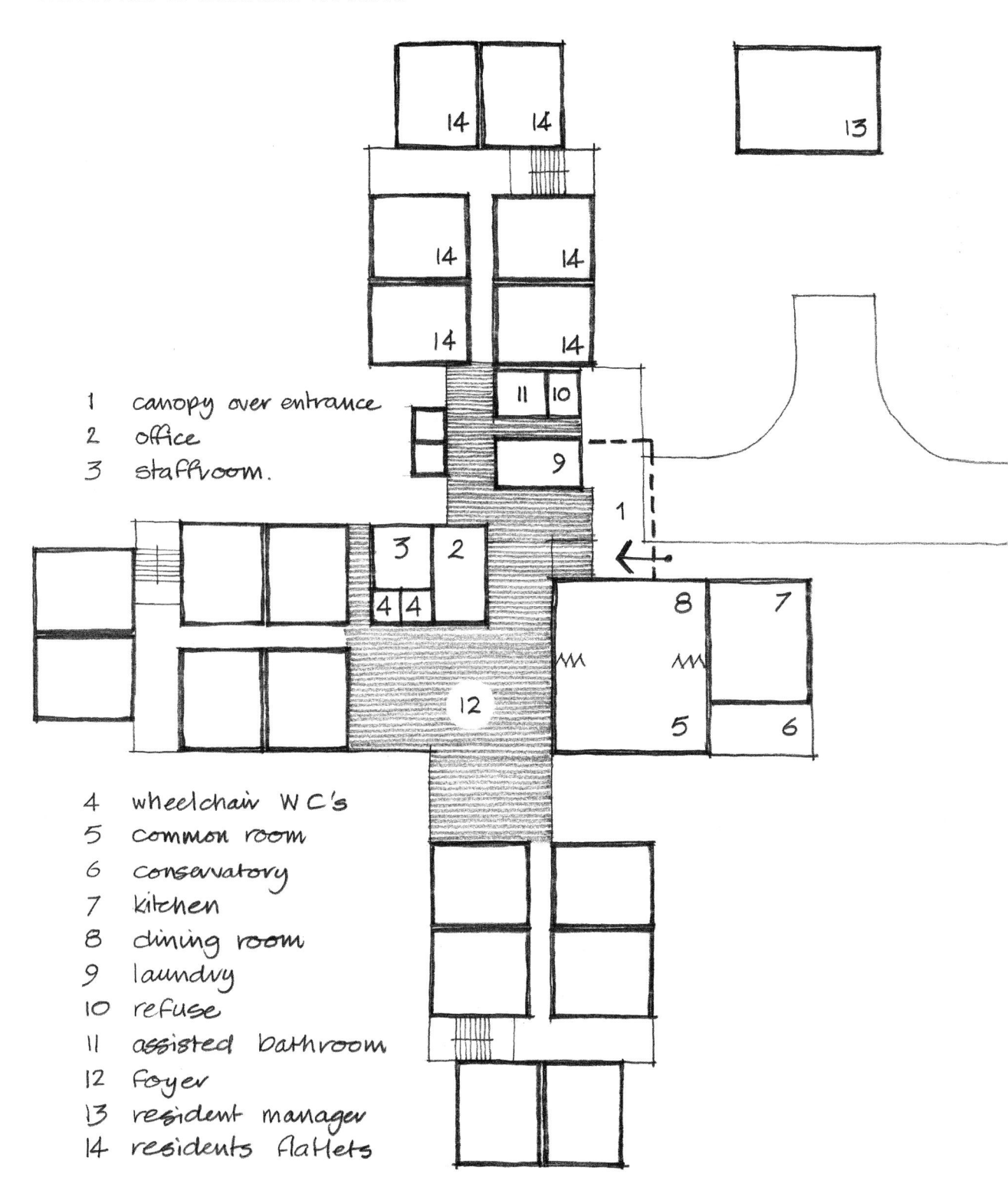

1 canopy over entrance
2 office
3 staffroom.

4 wheelchair WC's
5 common room
6 conservatory
7 kitchen
8 dining room
9 laundry
10 refuse
11 assisted bathroom
12 foyer
13 resident manager
14 residents flatlets

Fig. 5 Category 2½: Frail elderly 'hotel' model

CATEGORIES OF SHELTERED HOUSING

alternative methods of housing this group of people. We will now consider design parameters for the frail elderly.

For a definition of a frail elderly person requiring care, we consider the following profile[6] to be helpful and specific. A frail elderly person is:

> Someone who needs help at constant and frequent intervals with all or any of the following:
> (a) Getting in and out of bed
> (b) Dressing
> (c) Getting to the bathroom or lavatory
> (d) Moving about
> (e) Eating
> (f) Protection from a tendency to wander dangerously.

Fortunately most people do not deteriorate to this extreme and can cope, given the right environment, without the degree of care that can only be provided in a residential home. Frailty is not synonymous with inability to care for oneself.

The frail elderly are the most at risk of our clients. They fall over easily, suffering pain and injury, are apt to become disorientated and find that negotiating doors and stairs can be a problem. Cooking and housework can be difficult for them, but despite all these disabilities they can remain rational and creative people with the opportunity, in the right environment, of demonstrating to their family and friends how to grow old gracefully. The design of frail elderly accommodation should make this possible. The frail elderly require extra care of the sort that families were once able to offer to grandparents within the family. They also need to maintain a degree of privacy and independence.

Frail elderly schemes may adopt either the 'hotel' or 'grouped-unit' model. In the hotel model the warden, kitchen and dining room provision is centralised, with grouped sitting in public space more akin to a hotel foyer where social intercourse is optional. (See Figure 5.) The grouped unit disperses wardens, kitchens and dining rooms with adjacent common rooms; a typical layout for 40 people would provide four separate buildings of 10 units, each building having its own warden, and dining and common room facilities. (See Figure 6.) In considering the advantages and disadvantages of each model, Alison Norman[7] directs attention to the degree of privacy obtained and its effect on the community character: 'It seems likely that group antagonisms and inadequate staff could make life in a group unit much more severely unpleasant than in a home designed on the hotel model where incompatible people can easily avoid each other.'

For residents' privacy and independence, private flatlets or bed-sitting rooms are recommended, fitted out with a bath or shower room designed for easy access, and cooking equipment to enable them to prepare simple meals and beverages; this provides them with a home base for their own quiet enjoyment or for entertaining visitors. Examination and consultation with doctors or health agencies can also take place in the privacy of their own rooms. It is not necessary or desirable to introduce a separate consultation room within a scheme. Ease of mobility in the dwelling and throughout the building is essential.

Provision must be made within the building for dining and informal social interchange. Meals may either be cooked by staff or may be contracted out. Kitchen and dining space may be centralised or, as in the case of Abbeyfield Homes, dispersed to provide groups of 10 flatlets, each enjoying its own sitting, dining and kitchen facility.

The design of circulation space throughout the building should be such that the residents can move freely in well-lit areas. Complicated layouts should be avoided. For most residents the staircase will not be of much use in the event of fire, so that means of escape and fire protection must be carefully considered.

---

[6] Anchor Housing Association Policy Review Forum, 1981

[7] Norman, A., *Bricks and Mortals: design and lifestyle in old people's homes*, Centre for Policy on Ageing, 1984

CATEGORIES OF SHELTERED HOUSING

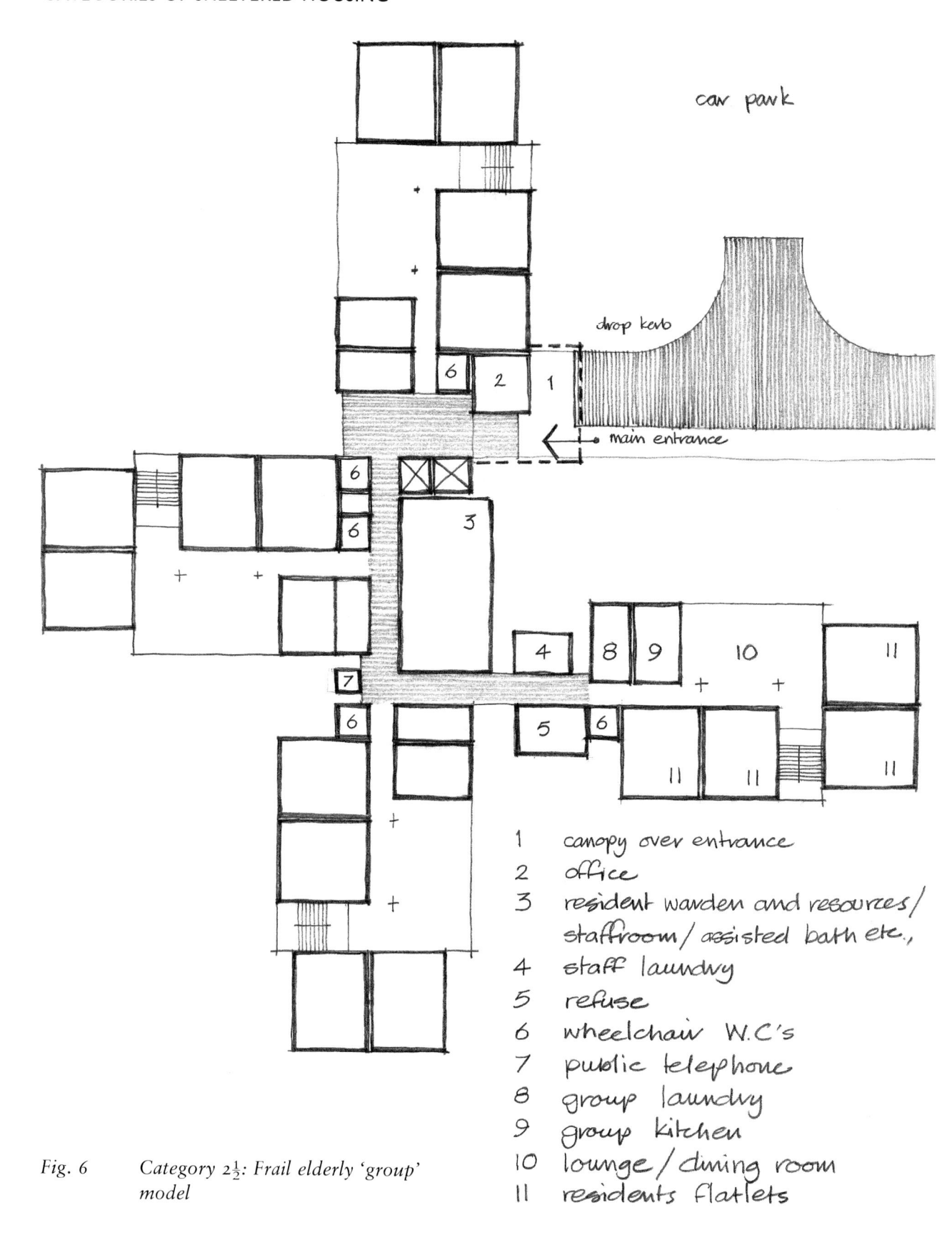

Fig. 6 Category 2½: Frail elderly 'group' model

1 canopy over entrance
2 office
3 resident warden and resources/ staffroom/assisted bath etc.,
4 staff laundry
5 refuse
6 wheelchair W.C's
7 public telephone
8 group laundry
9 group kitchen
10 lounge/dining room
11 residents flatlets

Conclusion

The clients come from a variety of socio-economic backgrounds: the disadvantaged moving from poor housing conditions to the warmth and companionship of their new home, 'empty nesters' seeking on retirement more convenient housing to enable them to live a full life in comfort, with varying degrees of background support. The location of the new home, its proximity to shopping and leisure facilities, friends and family, is of fundamental importance to all.

The ageing process does not lead inevitably to the surrender of all independence in a residential care home. Imaginative design, creating an environment sympathetic to the needs of people handicapped by infirmities, enables the elderly to lead independent lives. Experience has shown that, with the exception of psychotic neurosis, the infirmities of old age can be coped with in a sheltered framework of design and management, provided support services are arranged.

The different patterns of development, Categories 1, 2 and $2\frac{1}{2}$, have evolved from considerations of management and methods of funding development as much as in response to housing need. A generalised view of housing needs for the elderly would blur all these categories, but it is not sensible to categorise old people. If all houses were user-friendly, to borrow computer jargon, and close to shopping facilities, there would be no need for any category other than perhaps $2\frac{1}{2}$, housing the frail. Staying put would then be a practical option, but many houses are not suitable for conversion to use by the elderly and their location makes them impractical.

Whilst it is desirable to avoid 'ghetto' situations in large developments, there is further scope for schemes incorporating all the services that most elderly people come to require, a return perhaps to 'service' flats with restaurant and other facilities.

We have discussed the variables of service, privacy and scale of development, categorising different approaches to the subject. In the next chapter we shall look at the environment suitable for sheltered housing schemes.

3 SITE LOCATION, ENVIRONMENT, AREA, CAR PARKING AND SERVICES

Site location and environment

The suitability of a site and of its environment for sheltered housing must be carefully examined before a project is embarked on. The level of demand for this specialised form of housing should be ascertained and the appropriateness of the locality for the socio-economic group it is proposed to house considered.

In both publicly-funded and privately-financed schemes the proximity of peer groups, family and friends is important for the prospective resident. Social contact and activity helps to sustain independence whilst providing a sympathetic and supportive background. The market for sheltered housing is not unlimited, so the existence of a demand should be firmly established. Over-provision in any one area may bring competition, and poorly researched and designed schemes will fail, possibly coming back on to the market after refurbishment as housing for young people!

The criteria for site selection are considered below under the following headings:

1. Service and leisure facilities
2. Communications
3. Environment

Service and leisure facilities

For convenience of day-to-day living and involvement in local affairs there must be easy access to post office, bank, building society, shops, health centre, church, community centre, library, adult education centre and leisure facilities generally. Figure 7 illustrates the idea of 'sympathetic neighbours'.

The proximity of commercial centres providing facilities for obtaining pensions and cashing cheques, and of foodstores for day-to-day purchases, is of primary importance. It is essential that these enterprises are well established, with a secure economic future. The commercial failure of such facilities would invalidate the housing concept. This can be a problem in rural areas, where the advent of the motor car and shopping centres has undermined many village shops. Many dreams of retiring to an idyllic country village are thwarted by lack of basic amenities; our elderly are regrettably being directed as a result to town centres, with all the lack of security those entail.

Health care – medical, dental, optical – must be available locally to meet the needs of the elderly.

For many elderly people the move into sheltered housing has been prompted by bereavement. The community nature of sheltered housing will help combat loneliness and desolation, but outside agencies such as the church or community centre also have an important role to play.

Studies of mental stimulation of the elderly through further education (the 'University of the Third Age')[1] suggest that you *can* teach an old dog new tricks and that the resulting companionship is very beneficial. Senile dementia is not a necessary part of growing old and, incidentally, can affect young people too! Research into the diminution of mental faculties suggests that the changes are minimal. Part-time and evening

[1] Eric Midwinter, *Age is opportunity: education and older people*, Policy Studies in Ageing No. 2, 1982

SITE LOCATION, ENVIRONMENT, AREA, CARS & SERVICES

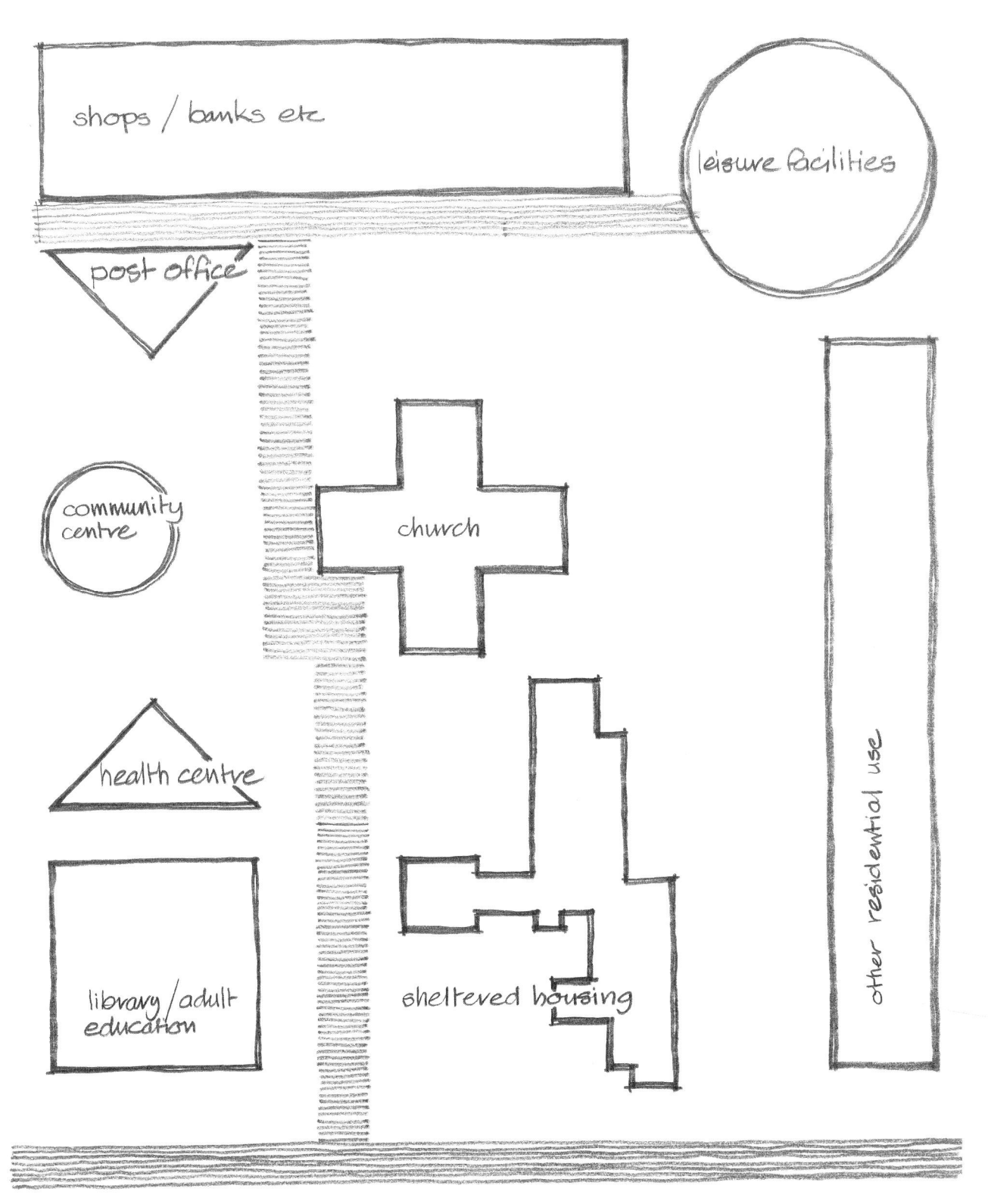

Fig. 7   Sympathetic neighbours. Sheltered housing sites should be close to all amenities in a sympathetic environment.

35

SITE LOCATION, ENVIRONMENT, AREA, CARS & SERVICES

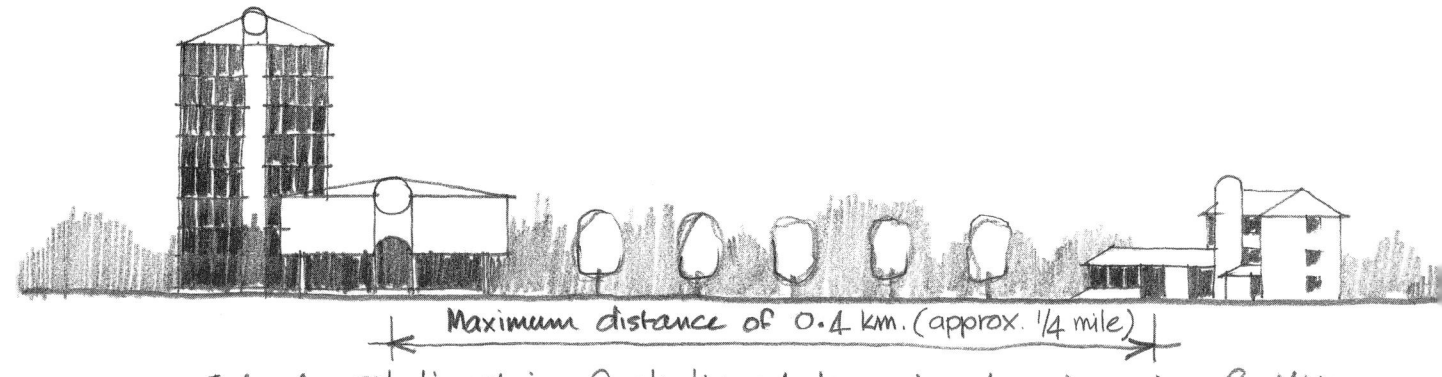

Maximum distance of 0.4 km. (approx. 1/4 mile)
Ideal relationship of sheltered housing to shopping facilities

Avoid routes traversing heavily trafficked roads

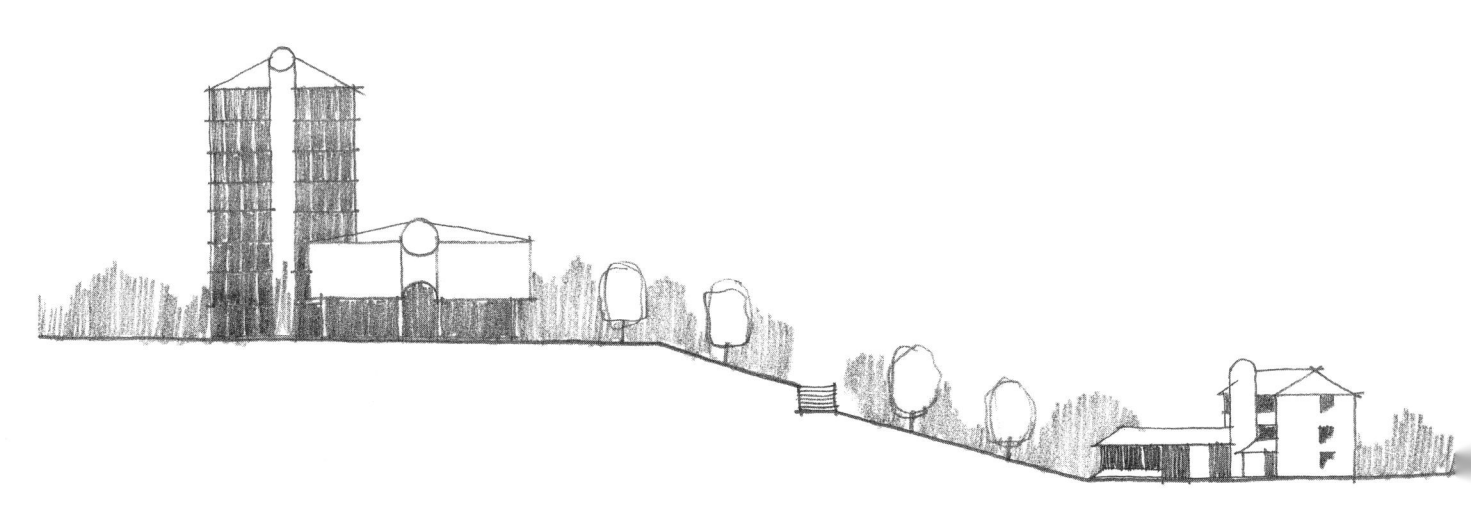

Avoid routes with steep inclines or steps

Fig. 8   Routes to shopping facilities

courses in a local Education Centre can provide opportunities for retired people to develop new interests or retain former hobbies and pursuits, keeping them mentally active and independent in spirit. It is therefore an advantage to have further education facilities nearby.

Leisure activities can range from passive pursuits such as cinema and theatre to active participation in swimming, bowls, golf, etc. The retired person, no longer bound to a work routine, has time to engage in a more active social life. The location of clubs for leisure activities, of libraries and places of further education, takes on new significance. Church groups, Women's Institutes, the Townswomen's Guild, drama groups, horticultural societies, floral clubs, local history groups, photographic societies, wine circles, arts and crafts, all offer social and leisure opportunities and can enrich the lives of the elderly.

Communications

Pedestrian ways and public transport

Easily traversed pedestrian routes to service and leisure facilities are essential. 0.4 km (approximately ¼ mile) from the site to these areas is about the maximum acceptable distance. The site location must not be such that roads with busy vehicular traffic have to be crossed to reach shops, etc. The topography must be considered as well: are there inclines or steps on the route, making the journey difficult or wearisome? The flatter the terrain, the more suitable it is for the elderly and infirm. (See Figure 8.)

Advancing years, with failing eyesight and reactions, preclude car ownership for many. A reliable local public transport system is therefore essential for journeys to friends and family, for return visits from them and for holidays.

Environment

In site selection the location of services and leisure facilities may be suitable and communications good, but there remains the immediate environment, or *genius loci*, of the site to be appraised. This we consider under three headings:

1. Residential scale and category of use
2. Sympathetic neighbours
3. Privacy and routes through the scheme

1. Residential scale and category of use

Key determinants in site selection vary according to the scale and category of sheltered housing proposed. Small scale developments for the independent elderly (Category 1) present fewer problems of integration with adjoining residential development for family and general use. Schemes of 10 to 20 units, without communal rooms, can be designed using normal residential design parameters, but with special regard to designing the communal landscaped areas carefully so as to provide 'defensible space' and mutual community supervision.

Large projects such as Category 2 schemes require sites and neighbourhoods where the scale of building can be sympathetically related to adjacent development. To meet the special needs of the elderly any development above ground floor level will require a lift, therefore the most economical development would be on three or more floors. The area of site required will depend on its location and the permitted density of development. Generally in suburban zones a density of 70 habitable rooms per acre would be appropriate. In inner city areas the density may be increased to 100+ habitable rooms per acre. The character of the site and its immediate environs should be sympathetic to the category of use proposed. The proposed buildings must be integrated by careful and sensitive design to avoid the appearance of a 'ghetto' for the elderly.

2. Sympathetic neighbours

'Sympathetic neighbours' would include other residential use, a community centre, a church, a library and a small-scale shopping centre, provided all are developments into which the scheme can easily be integrated and the residents can take part in community life.

Sites in well-established areas on the fringe of commercial centres, in the zone where shopping gives way to housing, are ideal for sheltered housing schemes. Unsympathetic neighbours to be avoided are:

Industrial plants, generating noise and smells.

Car parks to licensed premises or clubs where the noise of car engines revving up and doors slamming late at night will disturb the residents.

Playgrounds associated with schools for young children where the intensity of noise generated at play periods could be a nuisance. Contrary to popular belief, many elderly do not take kindly to being located where they can see the children play. Many have fond memories of their children but now feel that they have 'done their bit'.

Fire stations, hospitals and police stations and all premises where vehicular activity, accompanied by sirens, occurs day and night.

Airports, and flight paths to and from them.

Heavy traffic routes, road and rail, used day and night.

Unsupervised open spaces where young people congregate. Old people are particularly wary of young people; their rumbustiousness (or worse, violence) and peculiar modes of dress and conversation are not readily comprehended even by their parents – still less by their grandparents.

3. Privacy and routes through the scheme
Within the boundaries of the site the residents will require privacy for the quiet enjoyment of their dwellings. Ideally the site should have interesting views enabling visual contact with the outside world and activity. Residents should not be made to feel isolated. However, sites with rights of way over them should be avoided – the elderly want security from vandalism and burglary, and due account should be taken of the local crime rate. A London local authority's award-winning scheme failed to do so: a footpath was designed through the scheme to encourage 'community contact', but this only encouraged community glue-sniffing – by youngsters around the courtyard's feature, a central laundry. The footpath has since been stopped off and the residents feel safe enough to use their laundry again. Community contact is desirable but not when it threatens security.

Conclusion
The market demand for sheltered housing in a specific location needs careful assessment to ensure its commercial or social success. For public sector sheltered housing reference to the local authority housing list will assist in establishing the likely level of demand. For the future success of the scheme, local services, shops and transportation must be financially sound and assured.

The site environment should be suitable for the scale of development proposed, with sympathetic adjoining development. Privacy and security should be provided but not at the expense of isolation from the local community life.

Site area, car parks and services

Having discussed the suitability of a site and its environment for sheltered housing, we will now consider what area of land is required for different categories of housing, what provision should be made for car parking, and finally what services must be provided to the site.

Site area
Category 1 A small community, self-support group of 10 units in a rural or suburban context would require a site area of approximately 0.2 to 0.3 ha (0.5 to 0.75 acres). This area would have to be increased if the site contained special features limiting the development area, such as trees covered by a Tree Preservation Order. As a general rule a minimum road frontage of approximately 30 m (100 ft) is desirable in order to plan vehicular and pedestrian access satisfactorily into a courtyard development, supervised by the residents. In larger developments a density of 50 to 70 habitable rooms per acre would be appropriate to a rural or sub-rural area. Densities in inner city areas can be increased substantially as height restrictions fall away, and car parking requirements are reduced as public transport services improve.

SITE LOCATION, ENVIRONMENT, AREA, CARS & SERVICES

Category 2 The most frequent size of development, employing one warden servicing 30 dwellings, requires approximately one acre of land. Incremental increases in area must be allowed for additional units and warden provision. As in Category 1, for schemes in inner city areas the site size may be dramatically reduced.

Category 2½ Achievable densities of development are not increased for this category. The frail elderly will not have cars but extra provision must be made for staff and visitors. In addition, because of frailty, additional common space must be provided for kitchens, dining and sitting areas.

Cars and the elderly

Car ownership varies considerably. An analysis of its incidence[2] in publicly funded cost-rent sheltered flats managed by the Anchor Housing Association revealed that, from 8919 flats in 249 schemes, only 437 of the tenants owned cars (4.9%). The flats included in the survey were primarily Category 2.

For most Category 2 public sheltered housing schemes where the site is within walking distance of shops and public transport, a car parking ratio of one space to four dwellings is sufficient. For Category 1 public schemes, where the residents are presumed to be more active, this ratio should be increased to one space to three dwellings.

Baker and Parry,[3] reporting on car ownership by the elderly, quote developers McCarthy and Stone as advocating car parking ratios of one space to four dwellings and the Guardian Housing Association as recommending a ratio of one to three, with space reserved for upgrading it to a ratio of one to two should this be necessary. Some flexibility in allocating car parking space is desirable: the active elderly moving into a new scheme in a salubrious and wealthy neighbourhood are likely in some cases to need car parking in a ratio of one to one. As the community ages the car parking requirement will diminish, as individuals give up driving. All UK car owners over the age of 70 must re-apply every three years for a driving licence, with a declaration of fitness. This is the age at which many give up driving. Car ownership is clearly related, then, to health, wealth and site location.

In the private sector, the factors of site location and likely car ownership must be carefully considered, as there is a wide disparity in the statistical evidence. We recommend that provision should be made for most schemes at the ratio of one to two, in schemes catering for most elderly people, increasing to one to one for the affluent in out-of-town developments.

If this appears to be an overprovision the spaces can be landscaped initially and introduced into use as and when required. Car parking in Category 2½ schemes will only be required for staff and visitors at a ratio of one space to four in public schemes and one to three in private. (See Table 2.)

Table 2 **Car parking ratios**

	Dwelling		Car space
Public sheltered housing:			
Category 1	3	:	1
2	4	:	1
2½	4	:	1
Private sheltered housing:			
Category 1	1	:	1
2	2	:	1
2½	3	:	1

For inner city sites close to public communications and all facilities these car parking ratios can be considerably reduced. In rural areas the incidence of car ownership and parking requirements may be higher.

---

[2]'Car Parking Survey 1979', Anchor Housing Association (unpublished)

[3]Baker, S. and Parry, M., *Housing for sale to the elderly. 3rd report: a review of the retirement housing market and future trends*, Housing Research Foundation, 1986

SITE LOCATION, ENVIRONMENT, AREA, CARS & SERVICES

Car spaces/Garages

As they become less agile, the elderly need more room to manoeuvre and park cars. Car parking spaces 5.00 × 2.5 m (16 × 8 ft) should be provided with a reversing zone of 7.00 m (23 ft). Handicapped elderly will need room to transfer from the car to a wheelchair, preferably under cover. A dropped kerb should be provided from the car park compound on to the access footway for wheelchair users. Some elderly prospective purchasers may require a garage to house their equally elderly vintage car; if this cannot be provided a sale may be lost. The garage can usefully be considered as an extension of the dwelling, providing covered space in which to set up a work bench for hobbies and handicrafts. For this space to be useful electric power will need to be available, and standpipes for cleaning cars should also be provided.

Services

The following services should be available to the site:

Water
Electricity
Drainage – foul and surface water
Telecommunications
Gas

The capacity of these services should be checked before the site is acquired. Where a heavy demand on electricity is anticipated the electricity board may require space to build an electrical sub-station. In those rural areas where public sewage disposal facilities are not provided, the sewage may be dealt with via a septic tank if the ground porosity is adequate. Alternatively, small sewage treatment plants can be a satisfactory solution. The use of gas in sheltered housing is contentious as it is a source of possible accident; however, private purchasers may be put off if they find they cannot cook by gas, and certain ethnic minorities, cooking with a wok utensil, cannot cope with electric cooking due to its lack of instant response to temperature change, much needed in Indo-Chinese cooking. Fuel for heating and cooking is discussed in Chapter 6.

4 | DETAILED DESIGN GUIDANCE

In this chapter we consider the detailed design of the dwellings and of the ancillary activities and spaces to be found in sheltered housing schemes. It must be emphasized that the space standards given are minimum and are appropriate only for public housing. They would be inappropriate for many private schemes. In the private sector the potential resident will not be trading down, but will expect to be able to move in with his or her prized furniture collected over the years, with everything in its place and a place for everything.

A checklist of design notes is provided for guidance in Appendix A, p.000.

Dwellings and space standards

Space standards within the sheltered dwelling will vary according to the socio-economic group to be housed. Public housing recommended space standards for Category 1 and 2 dwellings are as follows:

Table 3 **Space standards (areas in m², followed by sq ft equivalents)**[1]

Minimum overall size	Cat. 1 (Flat)	Cat. 2 (Flat)	Cat. 1 (Bungalow)
1 person (bedsitter)	32.6 (350.9)	30 (322.9)	33* (355.2)

*Bedsitting room

Minimum overall size	Cat. 1 (Flat)	Cat. 2 (Flat)	Cat. 1 (Bungalow)
1 person separate bedroom	34 (366.0)	34 (366.0)	–
2 person one bedroom	47.5 (511.3)	41.5 (446.7)	48.5 (522.0)
3 person two bedroom	60 (645.8)	–	61 (656.6)

[1]Source: Ministry of Housing and Local Government Circular 82/69

The following descriptions of rooms, spaces and fittings are for Category 1 and 2 dwellings. Flatlets for the frail elderly will be described separately.

Entrance

The design of each flat should enable the residents to express their own personalities. This individual approach starts at the front door to the flat. A hole in the wall of a long corridor is not the most inviting entrance; a sense of place can be achieved by recessing the door off the approach and providing an adjacent delivery shelf. A large delivery shelf invites residents to display plants and ornaments and give free rein to their individuality. (See Figure 9.)

At the very least, the delivery shelf should be at least 100 mm (4 in) deep, sufficient to allow door-to-door deliveries of milk and bread to be left without causing a hazard by cluttering up the access routes. For the self-esteem and independence of residents, personal deliveries of post,

Fig. 9 Entrances to flats should be inviting and make it possible to personalise the access with plants and pictures. This example at Meachen Court, Wokingham, shows the key elements of the entrance door, delivery shelf and access to the electricity supply meter. Note the letter box positioned away from the lock: this security measure helps to frustrate intruders attempting to open the lock by way of the letter box. (Architects: Phippen Randall and Parkes. Photo: Crispin Boyle)

for instance, should be encouraged as centralised collection points smack of institutions.

Dwellings entered externally should have a canopy for weather protection. The entrance lobby should be at least 900 mm (36 in) wide and where possible this should be enlarged to 1200 mm (48 in). Provision should be made in the lobby for the storage of hats and coats, and a linen store is also most conveniently positioned in the lobby. Linen stores with access from bathrooms and kitchens are not entirely satisfactory because of the steam generated in these rooms. The linen store should be fitted with two or more slatted shelves between 600 and 1200 mm (24 and 48 in) above the floor level. Additional general storage should also be provided for suitcases, brooms, etc., with at least a couple of deep shelves 900 and 1400 mm (36 and 55 in) above floor level. The warden call speech unit may be situated in the lobby where space is sufficient. All internal lobbies should have borrowed natural light via a fanlight over the living room door. Where letter plates are fitted in entrance doors, provide a postal sack or wire basket to save residents stooping down to pick up the post. The wire basket will also foil attempts by intruders reaching through the letter box to the door lock. In addition, if a letter plate is provided in flats, the inner flap should be steel to satisfy fire regulations.

Care should be taken at the design stage to avoid door handles clashing and doors opening on to the warden speech unit, especially if the lobby space is restricted. Such is the nature of the construction of flats that service drops get determined early in the contract and can be a nuisance to rectify later on.

Front-door locks must be suitable for arthritic fingers. Small snibs are difficult to operate. A sensible solution is the use of a lock operated by a key externally and a lever handle internally, but provision for pulling the door shut externally must be made. The lock can also frustrate emergency access in response to alarm calls. This problem can be overcome by using an electronic door release mechanism operated by the alarm trigger mechanism.

DETAILED DESIGN GUIDANCE

Living room

Many residents will spend most of the day in their living room. It is important therefore to ensure that they can enjoy a lively and interesting outlook and that the proportions of the room should accommodate furniture comfortably, with space to move around unencumbered by inconvenient furniture positions. Circular 82/69 recommends a minimum width of 3000 mm (118 in) but in practice 3200 mm (126 in) has been found to be a better minimum width.

Window-sill heights and transoms should not obstruct views out for seated people and the furniture layout of the room should make access easy for opening and closing the window (Figure 10). The window design should permit ease of use, with latches suitable for arthritic fingers. Special care must be taken with ground floor windows to ensure that they can be locked for security; security latches are available which will hold the window open 50 mm (2 in) for ventilation and also frustrate any burglars (Figure

Fig. 10 *Living rooms should have an interesting view and access to the window latches should be easy. In this example at Cherry Tree Court, Harwell, note the location of the television by the external wall to permit daytime viewing without reflection from the window, also the location of power points 1 metre (3.25 ft) above the floor level to save bending down to operate the switch.* (Architects: Francis Weal & Partners. Photo: Alan Williams)

DETAILED DESIGN GUIDANCE

Fig. 11 Ground floor windows should be fitted with security latches which are easy to operate, to provide ventilation and security. (Photo: Alan Williams)

DETAILED DESIGN GUIDANCE

living room must not about neighbouring bedroom or noise generating services

unobstructed access to window
telephone located by sitting area
television positioned for daytime viewing

600

sitting area - space for settee/easy chairs and chairside tables

kitchen door to open in direction of access route.

kitchen light switch

warden call speech unit
note: in 2 person dwellings position in lobby

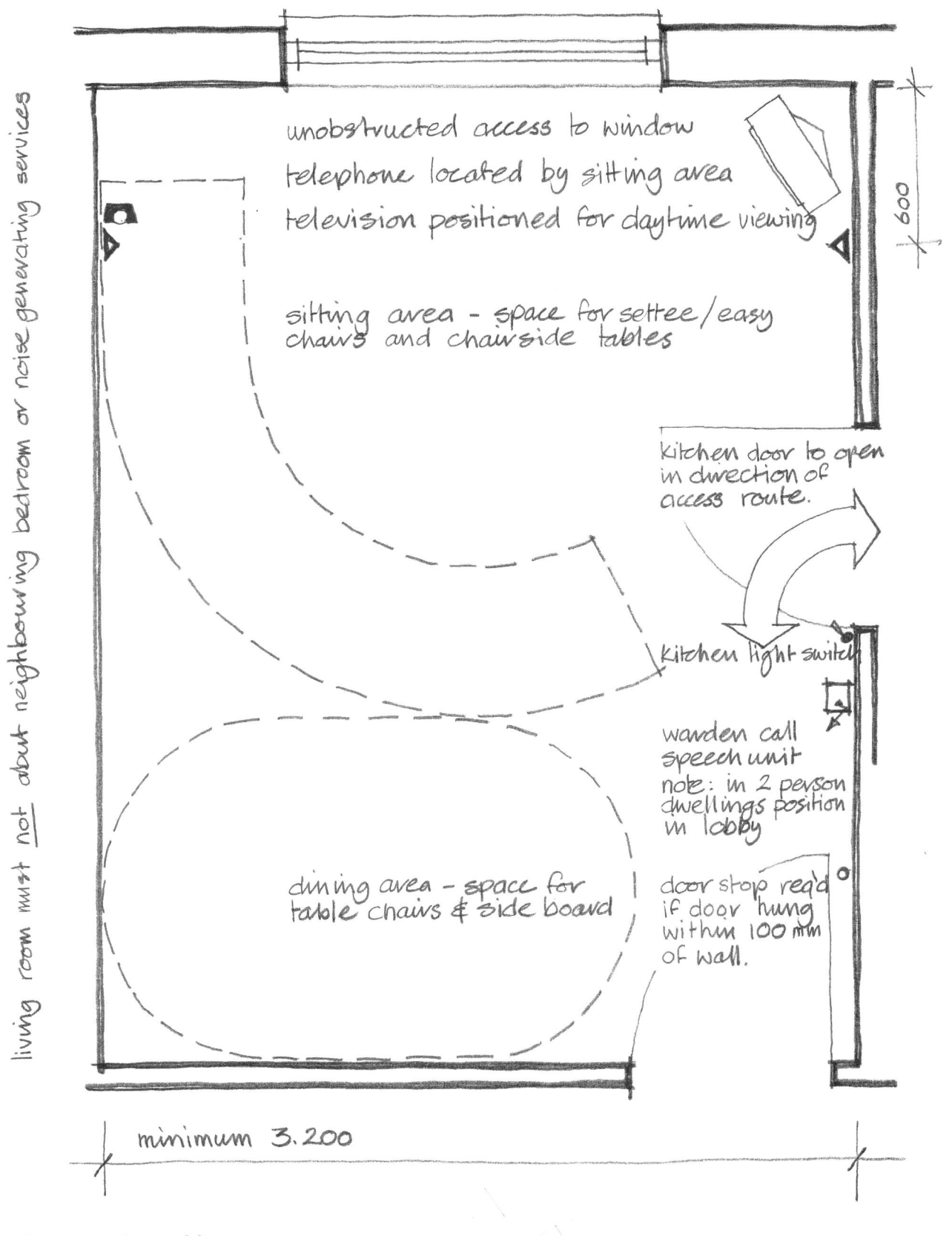

dining area - space for table chairs & sideboard

door stop req'd if door hung within 100mm of wall.

minimum 3.200

Fig. 12   Typical living room

DETAILED DESIGN GUIDANCE

11). The opening lights to upper windows should be at a safe distance for anyone leaning out to reach the closing gear. Within the room there must be space for at least two easy chairs or a settee and two easy chairs, chair-side tables for cups, newspapers, spectacles, and a reasonable amount of other furniture. The television location should be arranged to permit daytime viewing without the need to draw curtains to prevent light reflecting from the screen.

The dining table and chair should be positioned to permit easy access for the resident from the kitchen. Most residents will use a folding or gateleg table suitable for two to eat at normally and opening up for additional guests. In one-person dwellings the warden call speech unit is best positioned in the living room, by the door to the kitchen on the latch side. This in turn should be nearest to the entrance door to keep the route for carrying shopping to the kitchen as short as possible. Figure 12 illustrates the design details to be considered in the room layout and access route to the kitchen.

Kitchen

The kitchen must adjoin the dining area for ease of carrying food to the table. In two-person dwellings, the kitchen must be designed to include space for a small dining table and two chairs. This table is useful for informal meals and the preparation of food whilst sitting. Indeed, many women wish that architects allowed for a kitchen table as a matter of course as a good kitchen table is the right height for pastry-making and a boon to weary legs. There is a strong preference for kitchens to be on external walls with natural light and ventilation. However, in single-banked

Fig. 13   With single-banked corridor schemes, internal kitchens with a view out over the corridor can be very successful. This example at Meachen Court illustrates further the possibilities of personalising the resident's domain when viewed from the corridor. Note the lever taps which are easy to use. (Architects: Phippen Randall and Parkes. Photo: Crispin Boyle)

Fig. 14 Kitchen fittings should not be positioned under ventilating windows: in this example at Cherry Tree Court they are arranged on party and internal walls. Most kitchen equipment is 900 mm (3 ft) high, therefore base units should be the same height. Generally base units should be 500 mm (1.66 ft) deep. Note that ample worktop space should be provided either side of the cooker and that taps should be of a pattern easy for arthritic fingers to turn. (Architects: Francis Weal & Partners. Photo: Alan Williams)

corridor schemes internal kitchens can be successfully designed with views out through the corridor to the outside world (see Figure 13), but mechanical extract ventilation must then be provided. Internal kitchens also help designers to provide easier routes to the dining table and a better frontage for living rooms and bedrooms.

Kitchen fittings and furniture must not hinder ease of access for operating external windows; the most suitable opening light is a top-hung fanlight which can be left ajar in rainy conditions to permit ventilation without the ingress of rain. The kitchen layout of fittings and equipment should follow the sequential arrangement of storage, preparation and cooking. Circular 82/69 recommends a minimum space standard for kitchen storage of 1.7 m³ (60 cu ft) in one and two person flats, with the refrigerator forming part of this storage. It also recommends a kitchen worktop height of 850 mm (33 in) or less though in practice this is not convenient as most equipment, cookers, refrigerators and washing machines are designed to fit in with units 900 mm (36 in) high. Ideally, worktops should not be deeper than 500 mm (20 in) but as most equipment such as cookers and refrigerators is designed to fit into 600 mm (24 in) deep units, it is more practical to design for 600 mm (24 in) deep worktops.

Kitchen worktops must be provided on either side of the sink and cooker position. The worktop between the sink and cooker will be used most and the surface finish should be capable of withstanding hot pans and dishes (Figure 14). Sink taps must be easy for the elderly to operate. Kitchen units and fittings generally must be selected for safety and ease of operation. All activities in the kitchen involving hot dishes, steam and heat put the elderly at risk.

DETAILED DESIGN GUIDANCE

One person kitchen

- do not run pipes behind cooker or position windows over fittings.
- wall units over
- minimum 1 000
- 500
- note: worktop either side of cooker
- unobstructed access to window.
- refrigerator under worktop - ensure door swings fully open for removal of ice tray.
- fire blanket on wall to latch side of door.
- door to open in direction of access route

Two person kitchen

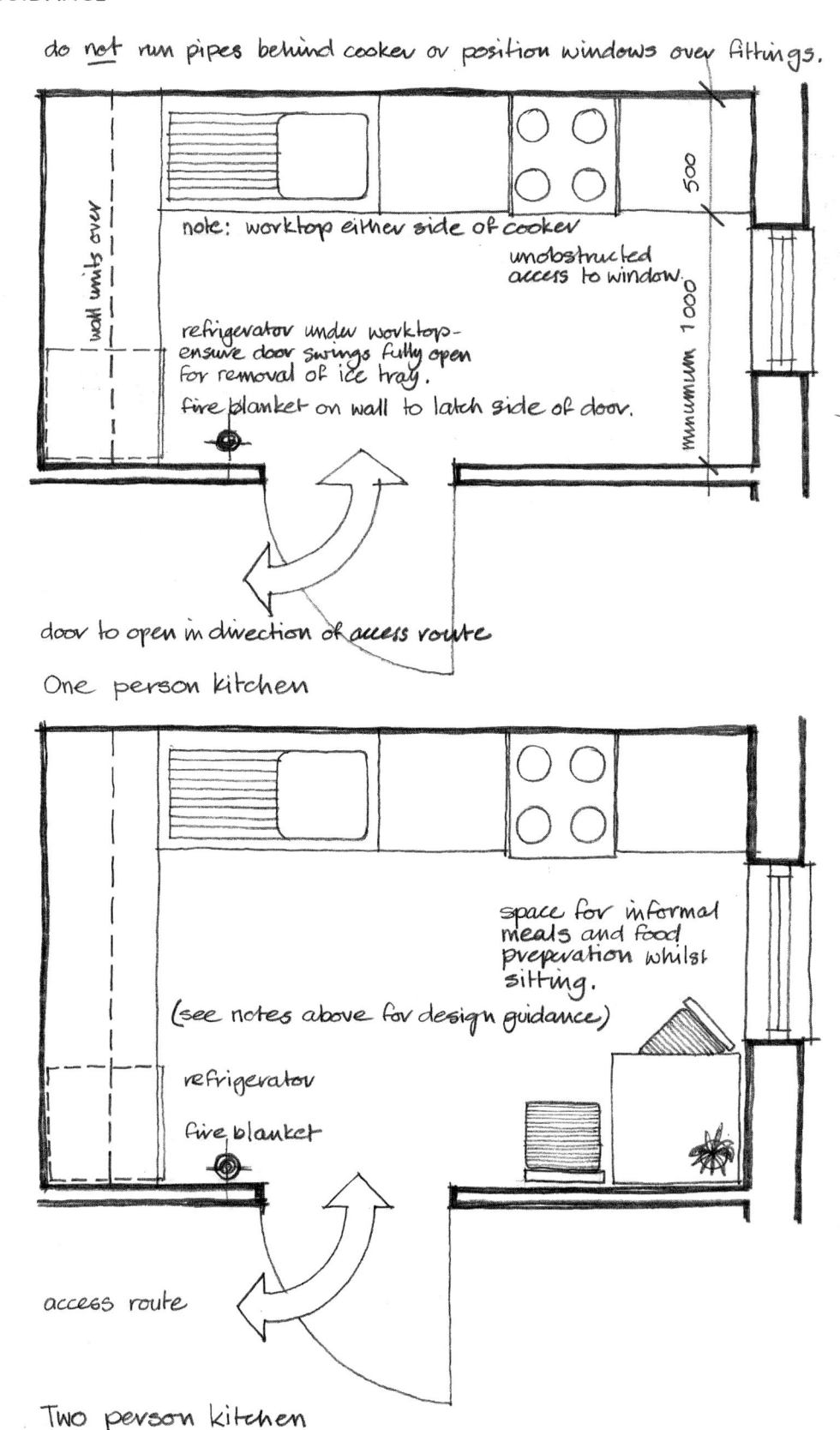

- space for informal meals and food preparation whilst sitting.
- (see notes above for design guidance)
- refrigerator
- fire blanket
- access route

Fig. 15 Typical Category 2 kitchens

Storage units below the worktop frequently involve getting down on hands and knees to fetch commodities or dishes, then rising from this position, and any wall cupboard door left open can inflict a painful injury. Where possible storage below the worktop, in drawer or tray units, is preferable, and the hazard of wall cupboards can be overcome by using sliding doors. On the subject of wall storage, circular 82/69 recommends that no shelf should be more than 1500 mm (60 in) above floor level.

It is impossible to provide hard and fast rules for the design of kitchens for wheelchair users, other than that the mounting height and disposition of equipment should be flexible to take account of whatever disability the incoming resident may have to cope with.

Where space and finance permit, split-level cooking hobs and ovens are safest. Electricity is the safest energy for the elderly to cook by but many people, including some ethnic minorities, will want gas. As fire is a hazard in the kitchen, a fire blanket should be provided on the wall by the latch side of the kitchen door.

Designers must ensure that there is enough room to allow doors to units and equipment to open fully and that these doors are hung to open in the right direction for ease of access. Ensure for example that the refrigerator door is properly handed and will open wide enough to facilitate the removal of ice trays, and that base unit drawers are not prevented from opening fully by low-level projecting window-sills. As a general rule there must be a minimum of 1000 mm (40 in) clearance between fittings.

Strong lighting is essential in the kitchen, and fluorescent lighting is best to avoid having shadowed areas. Care should be taken in the disposition of electric socket outlets. The UK Institute of Electrical Engineers' Regulations forbid the placing of sockets such that someone with one hand in sink water can touch an electric outlet with the other. The small size of these kitchens means that this must be considered carefully.

The relationship of sink to waste water stack must be such that the waste pipe does not run behind the cooker, causing the cooker to project forward of the base units.

Figure 15 illustrates typical one- and two-person kitchens.

Bedroom

Bedrooms must be isolated from noise. The bedroom wall should not adjoin the living room of another dwelling where a resident may be watching television with the volume turned on full due to hearing difficulties. Periods of being confined to bed are not infrequent with the elderly, so the outlook from the bedroom should be pleasant and window-sills low enough to permit a view of the outside world from the bed. The security arrangements should be similar to those for the living room windows. In two-person flats it is worth considering having sliding doors between the bedroom and the living room. This enables a couple to enjoy each other's company while one is confined to bed.

The recommended minimum floor space for single bedrooms is 8 m² (86 sq ft) and for double bedrooms 12 m² (130 sq ft). The single bedroom must be proportioned so as to permit full access around the bed for ease of bedmaking. Elderly backs should not be allowed to strain by having to stretch across the bed or 'hump' furniture around. In addition, there should be space for a wardrobe at least 600 mm (24 in) wide, a bedside table and a small dressing table and chair. The two-person bedrooms should be designed similarly to permit the room to be furnished with two single beds, with space between and beside the beds to facilitate bedmaking. Space should be available for a wardrobe at least 1200 mm (48 in) wide, two bedside tables, a small dressing table, a chest of drawers and a chair.

Bedrooms should be fitted with a warden alarm call point. The position of ceiling pull cords in relation to bedheads and the principal factors in designing the bedroom are illustrated in Figures 16 and 17.

DETAILED DESIGN GUIDANCE

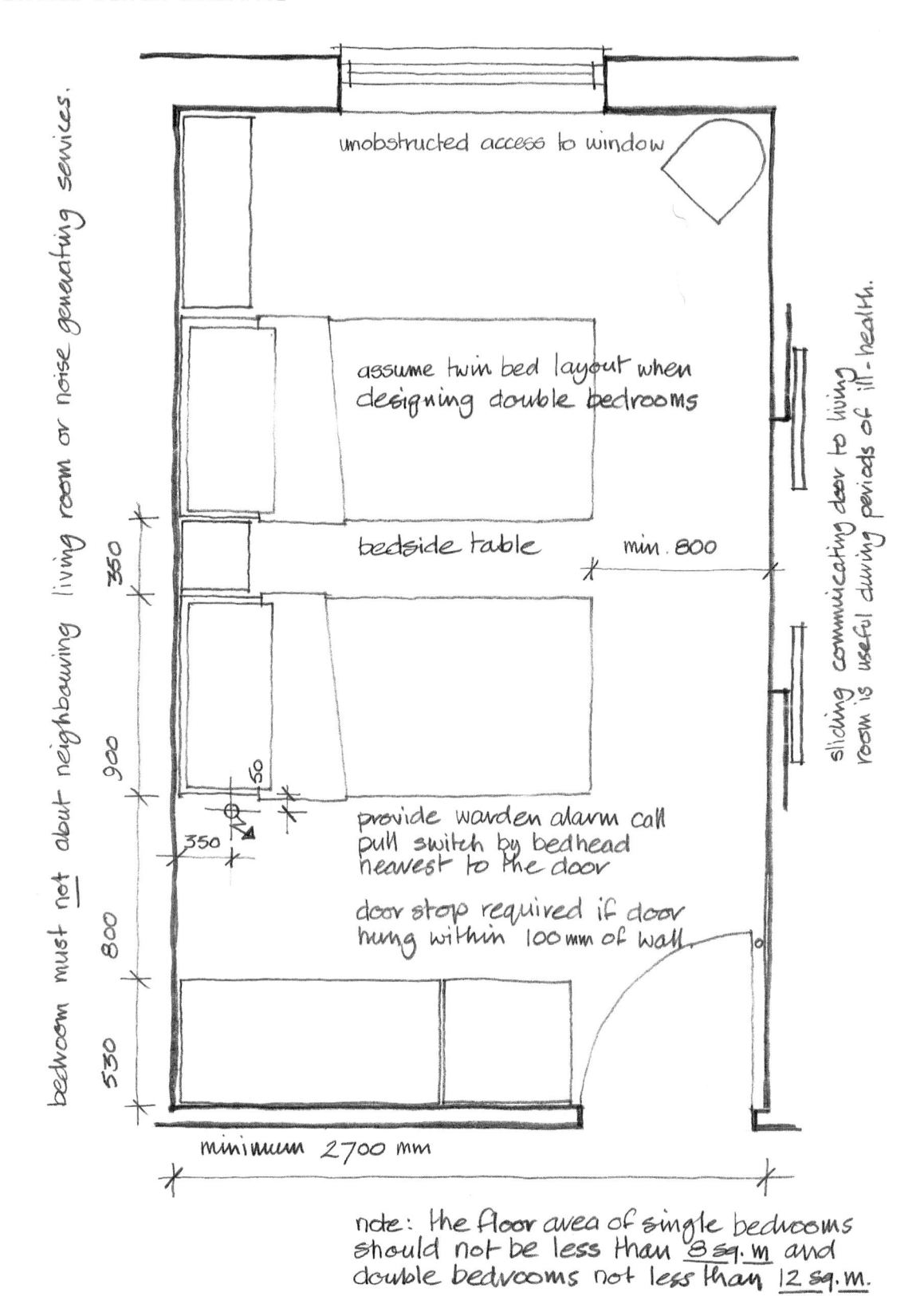

Fig. 16   Typical double bedroom

DETAILED DESIGN GUIDANCE

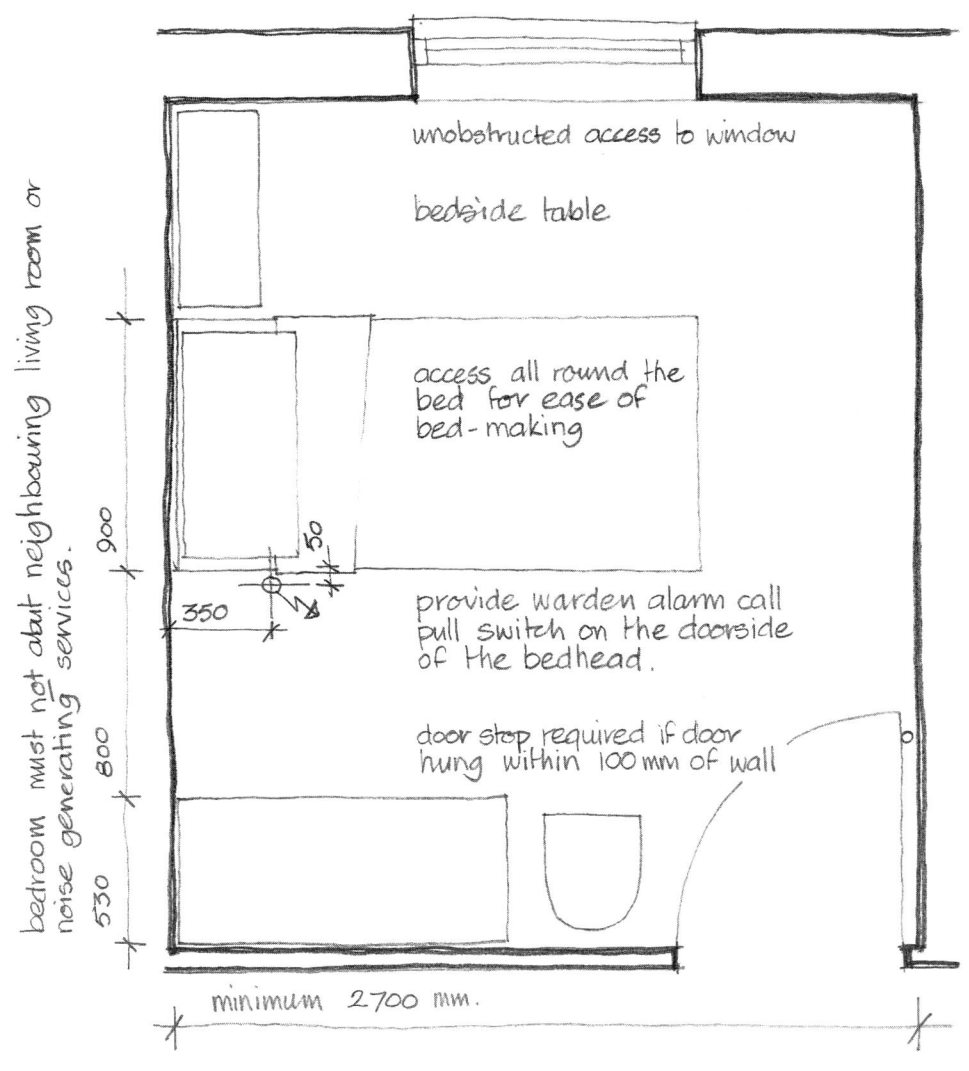

Fig. 17 Typical single bedroom

Bathroom

The minimum size for a bathroom should be 2200 × 1525 mm (87 × 59 in). In bathroom design an early decision must be made on what size bath to plan for. Circular 82/69 recommends that baths longer that 1550 mm (60 in) should not be used because of the danger of an elderly person, suffering a seizure or accident, slipping under the water and drowning. However, this size may not satisfy a potential purchaser used to a 1700 mm (66 in) length bath. Getting into and out of baths can be difficult for the elderly and for this reason lowline baths have been used in many schemes. Residents complain, however, that the water level in these baths is insufficient. A compromise is to use a standard bath employing a lowline trap with the bath mounted on the structural floor, 50 mm (2 in) below the finished floor level; this positions the bath floor a few millimetres above the finished floor level (Figure 18).

The hand basin should be mounted 810 mm above the floor level and be secure enough to withstand the weight of a resident leaning on it. The taps for baths and wash basins, as in the case

DETAILED DESIGN GUIDANCE

of the sink taps, must be easy to operate. This does *not* necessarily mean large 'disabled' lever taps – a tricorn or capstan spindle head is easy to operate for most people, and ceramic discs instead of washers allow the taps to be operated without undue effort or their being left dripping. WCs should be positioned a minimum of 400 mm (16 in) and a maximum of 450 mm (18 in) away from a side wall to leave room for a wall grab rail and lavatory roll holder. Grab rails will generally be

DETAILED DESIGN GUIDANCE

Fig. 18 Getting in and out of the bath can be difficult for the elderly. Disabilities vary and movement aids for one person may not be suitable for another. The standard solution shown here of a cranked bar behind the bath and a straight bar at the bath head has been found suitable for most users. Note the tricorn tap heads. Also the warden alarm pull cord designed to hang beside the bath but looped over the grab rail.
(Photo: Alan Williams)

required beside the WC and the bath. Where grab rails are not to be provided (potential purchasers may not wish to be reminded of potential infirmity) then designers should ensure that adequate fixing points are built into the structure to enable these mobility aids to be fitted if and when required. Do not use spring-loaded lavatory roll holders, as arthritic fingers cannot operate them: use a simple open-ended holder.

Mechanical air extraction is common in most schemes but where a window is provided then there must be easy and unimpeded access to the window gear; windows must *not* be installed over baths. The bathroom should be equipped with a towel rail, a cloak hook and a medicine cupboard. Do *not* position medicine cupboards over wash basins unless they can be fully recessed to prevent head injuries when rising from washing. A ceiling-mounted warden alarm cord must be provided in the bathroom by the bath. An alternative trigger point for emergency alarms can take the form of a 'panic button' beside the bath below bath rim. These 'panic buttons' however might prove difficult to find in an emergency.

All bathrooms must be fitted with outward opening doors whose locks can be opened from outside in an emergency. The reason for insisting on outward opening doors is that, should someone collapse behind the door, it could otherwise be difficult for anyone coming to the rescue to obtain access. Sometimes this can cause difficulties with local authorities who may not wish to see a door opening into the 'escape route'.

The problem can be overcome by persuasion and by siting the door swing so that it opens in the direction of egress. The bathroom floor must be non-slip.

The assumption has been that baths will be installed, but as showers become more popular (and indeed, are insisted upon by scrupulous Asians and Chinese) the case for them becomes stronger. The obstacle course that the elderly face in order to wash all over is absurd: in order to bath they are asked to step over a wall some 500 mm (20 in) high and sit down on the ground. The heavy emphasis placed generally on avoiding steps in a sheltered scheme is a further powerful argument in favour of showers.

Figures 19 and 20 illustrate alternative bathroom layouts.

Orientation and aspect

All flats should be designed so that at least the living room or principal bedroom enjoys a minimum of three hours sunshine per day throughout the year. With decreasing mobility it is important that living rooms should have an interesting and pleasant view. Judgements on the quality of view vary. For some clients a peaceful pastoral view is ideal, while others prefer to have a window on the world so that they can see the bustle of activity and feel in touch.

Extra-care units

As previously discussed, a recurring problem for the elderly is periods of ill-health when they are unable to care for themselves, and family or friends cannot provide the support they need. Transfer to a nursing home is one option, but because of the institutional nature of such establishments the patient may rapidly lose all independence and will not successfully return to independent living. Another option is to provide an extra-care unit within the sheltered housing scheme, for short-term use followed by convalescence in the resident's own flat. During the period of extra care the resident can enjoy visits from neighbours and friends and not feel isolated from normal life, secure in the knowledge that the flat is close at hand for them to return to.

DETAILED DESIGN GUIDANCE

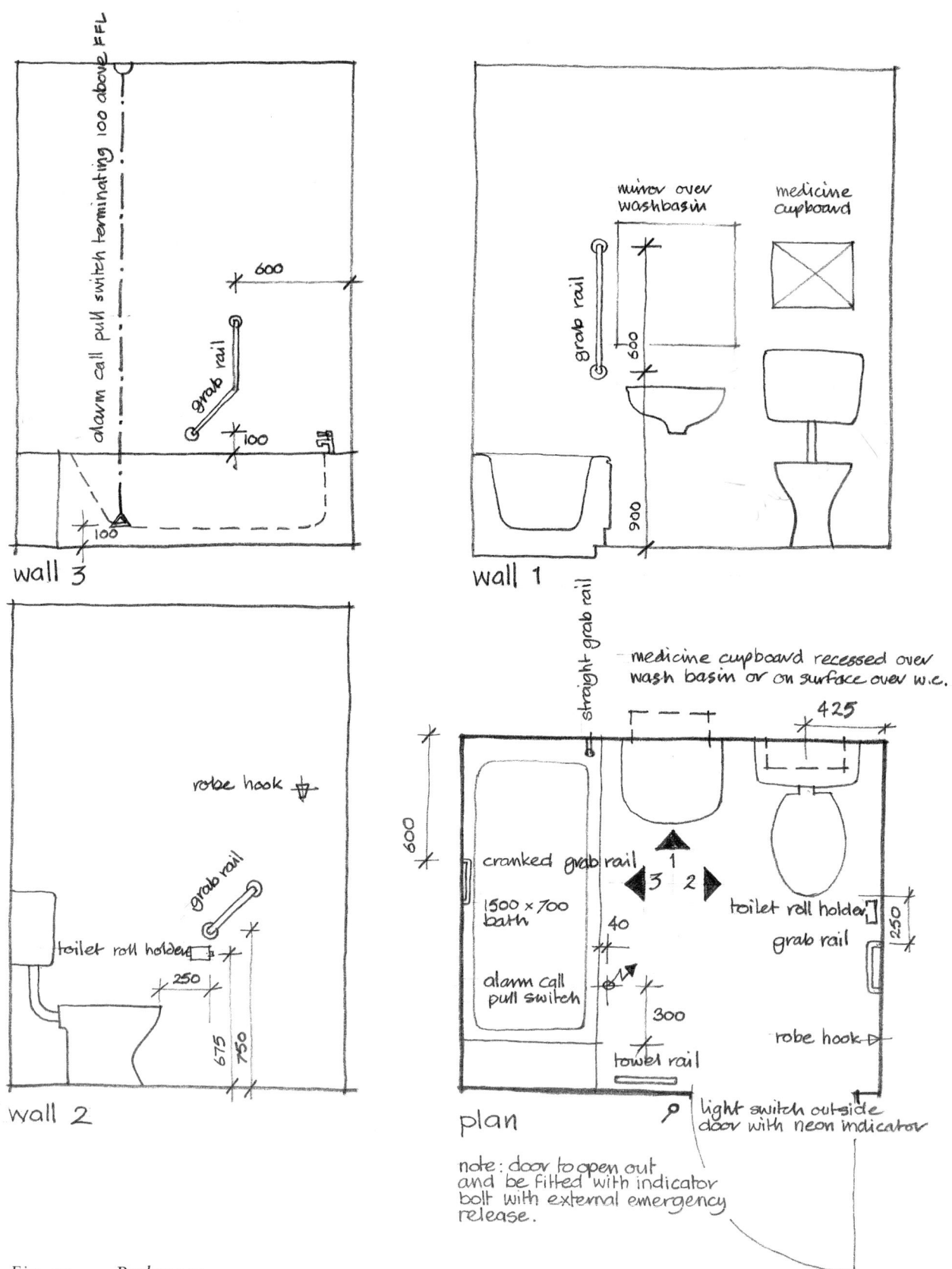

Fig. 19   Bathroom

DETAILED DESIGN GUIDANCE

Extra-care units should provide a bedroom for the patient, with an adjoining 'assisted' bathroom, a room for staff stopping overnight and a pantry for preparing meals. The orientation and aspect of the bedroom should allow the bed-fast person to enjoy sunlight and an interesting view. A warden call speech unit by the bedhead will keep the patient in touch.

An 'assisted' bathroom is a bathroom designed to allow someone who is frail to have a bath, with another person assisting them. It can usefully be planned off a lobby approach so that the 'assisted' bath facility may be used by other residents. The bathroom should be large enough to accommodate an island bath with space either side for lifting equipment. The lifting equipment is a seat, or cradle, designed to lift the person into the bath. The bath should be large enough to accommodate the cradle seat and should be set high to avoid straining the assistor's back – an occupational hazard for nurses. The bathroom should also be equipped with a WC, with space either side for transferral from a wheelchair, and a wash basin.

Figure 21 illustrates a typical 'assisted' bathroom.

Extra-care units, where they are provided, should be planned near the warden or ancillary staff accommodation for ease of supervision and response to emergency calls.

Frail elderly schemes

Hitherto little provision in the UK has been made for the frail elderly – those unable to cope with independent living but not so decrepit mentally or physically that a nursing home is the only solution. The concept of a 'Frail Elderly', or Category 2½ scheme, postulates the idea that given extra services, meals and peripatetic nursing the elderly can still retain their independence in a simple bed-sit flat.

The Abbeyfield developments of grouped units, each of ten residents with a housekeeper and communal kitchen, dining and sitting room space, are an example of frail elderly housing offering shelter and care.

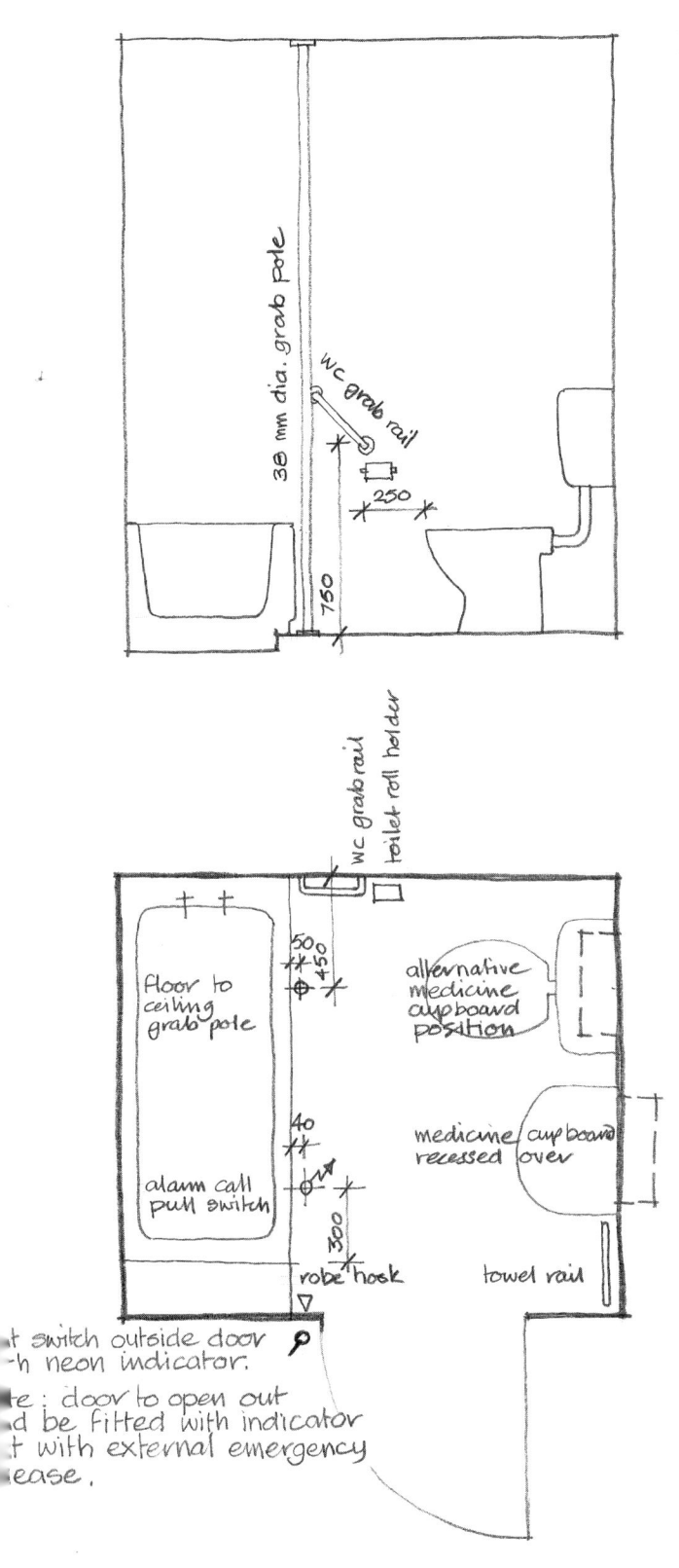

Fig. 20   Alternative bathroom layout

DETAILED DESIGN GUIDANCE

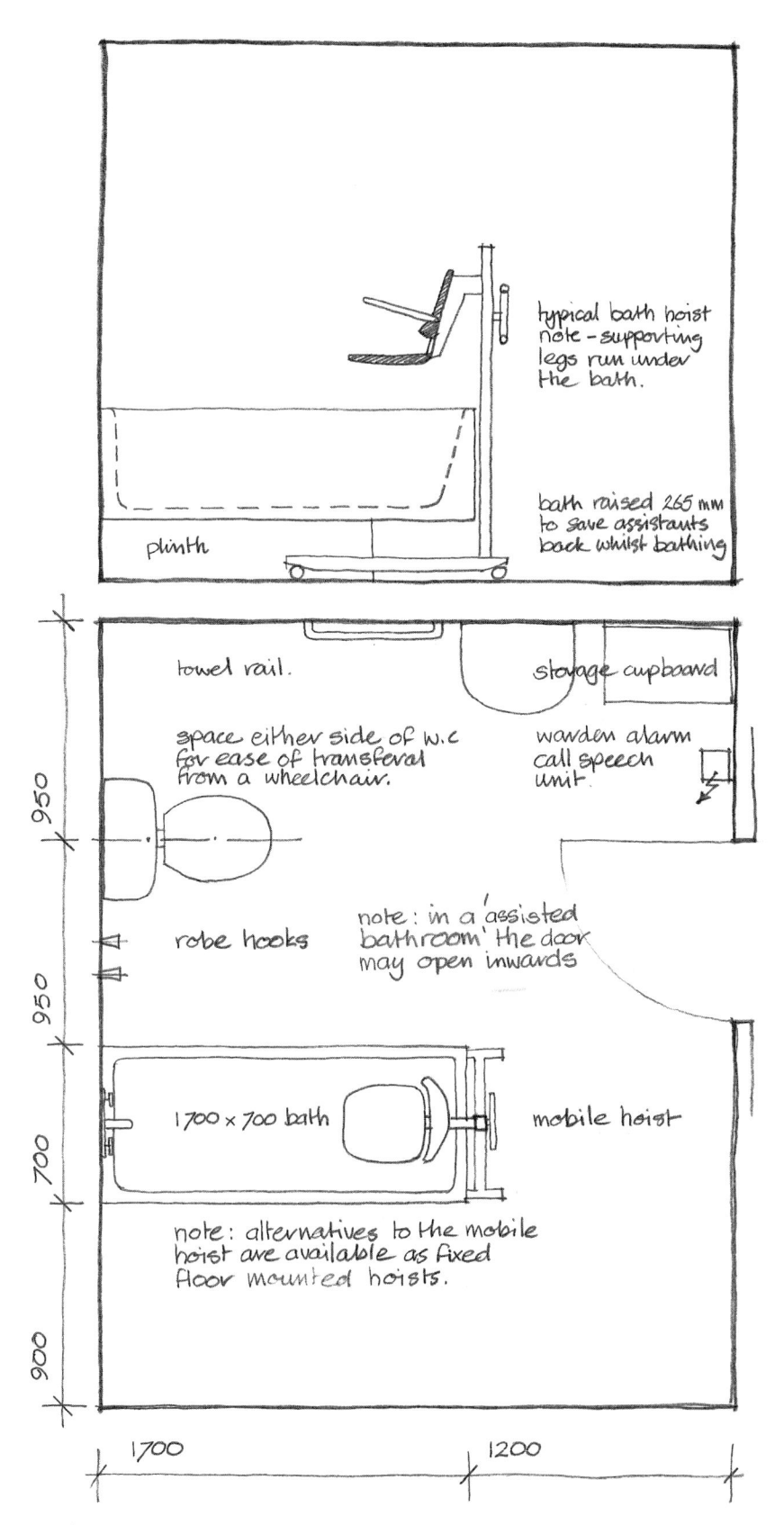

Fig. 21   Typical 'assisted' bathroom

DETAILED DESIGN GUIDANCE

Fig. 22 *An Abbeyfield bed-sitting room.*
(Architects: Phippen Randall and Parkes)

The Abbeyfield objective is to create a family-house, supportive atmosphere in which the residents can maintain a measure of independence, with a resident housekeeper assisting in the preparation of two main meals daily. The bed-sitting rooms do not have bathrooms but are fitted with a wash basin set into a floor unit, with a

DETAILED DESIGN GUIDANCE

KEY
1 common room
2 dining room
3 office
4 kitchen
5 laundry
6 telephone
7 w.c
8 refuse
9 assisted bathroom
10 sitting area
11 guest room
12 staff room
13 boiler room
14 hairdressing
15 managers flat
16 relief managers flat

RIVERS STREET

SOMERS ROAD

vehicle entrance

Plan 1a Housing for the frail elderly at Portsmouth: Ground floor and site plan

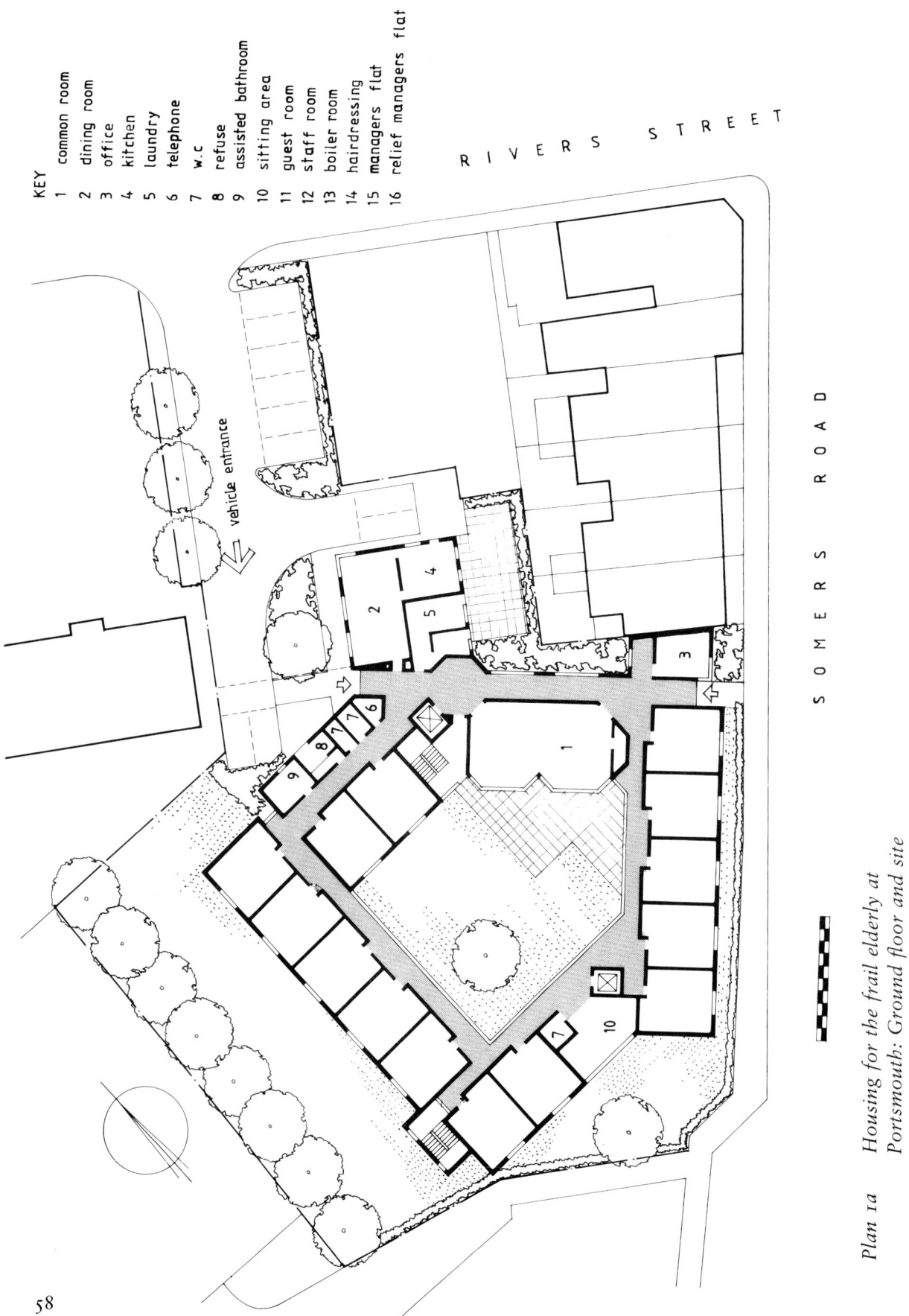

58

DETAILED DESIGN GUIDANCE

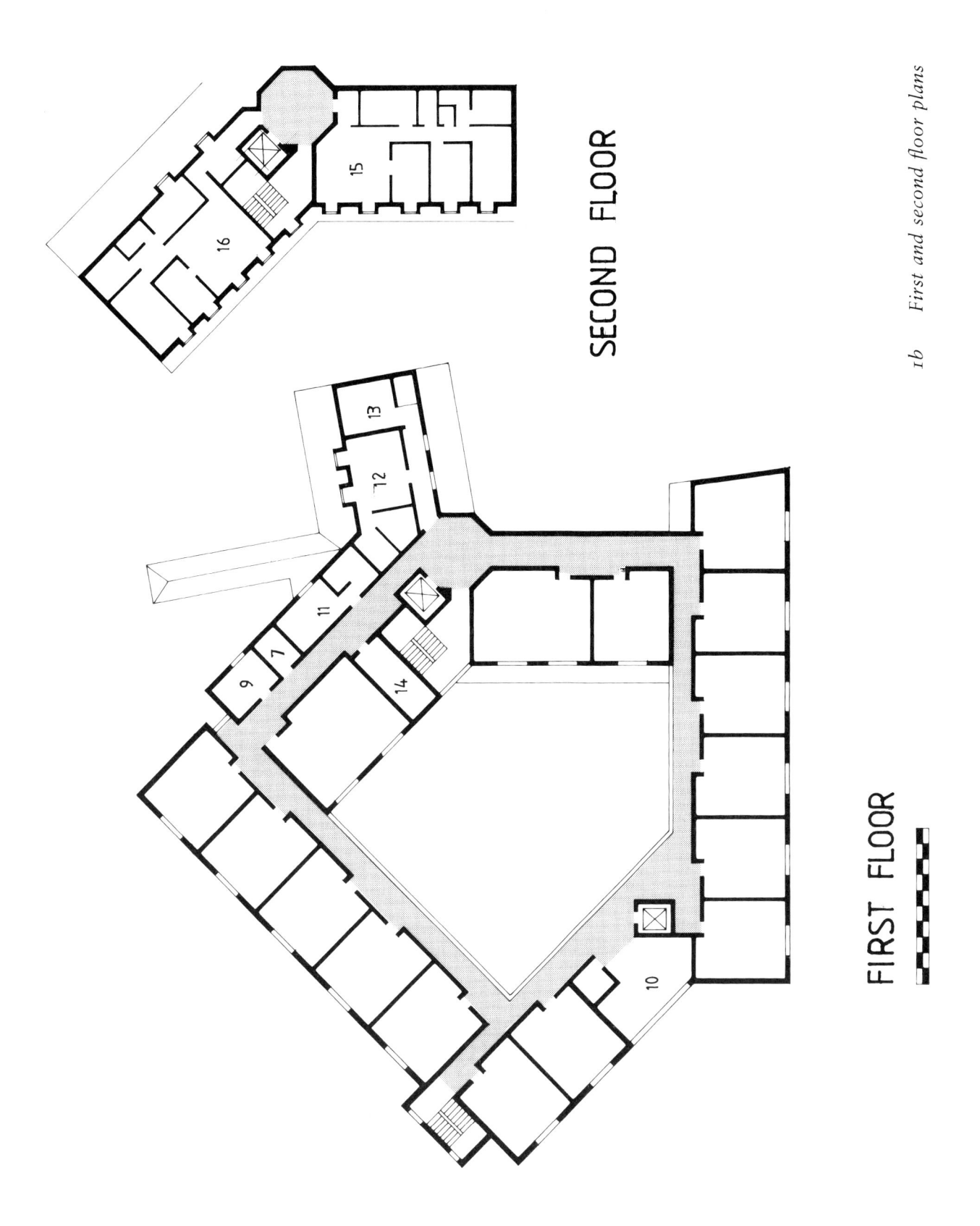

1b First and second floor plans

SECOND FLOOR

FIRST FLOOR

59

DETAILED DESIGN GUIDANCE

mirror over and adjacent worktop space for a kettle and toaster. The floor space of these Abbeyfield bed-sitting rooms is approximately 17.5 m² (188.4 sq ft). (See Figure 22.)

The housing concept is a dispersed Group Model with each group of ten units being autonomous. Whilst creating a 'family' atmosphere the dispersed groups suffer the disadvantage that it is uneconomic to provide a lift for each group, thus restricting the use of the first floor to fully mobile residents. As discussed earlier (p.ooo), when considering the pros and cons of 'hotel' or 'grouped-unit' models, the latter schemes in 'family'-orientated designs can also lead to friction due to lack of privacy in the public spaces. Successful 'family' schemes must depend upon careful resident selection and a sympathetic and diplomatic housekeeper.

There is a trend towards providing greater opportunities for independence and privacy for the frail elderly in very sheltered housing. This development, emerging from experience of Category 2 schemes, is frequently referred to as Category 2½. The hypothesis[1] is that with more convenient flats, and supporting services brought in, the frail elderly can still enjoy an independent life-style. The Portsmouth project (Plan 1) is an example of the movement towards bed-sit flats, each having their own bathroom and a centralised control or management unit. This project is designed on the 'hotel' model. The control or management unit will require 24-hour staffing, a support service which can only operate through shift work. Staff need not live in, but for continuity a resident housekeeper or warden is desirable.

The bed-sit flat

The bed-sit flat is the resident's own domain where he or she may express their own personality and retain a degree of independence not found in a nursing home. The keynote of the design should be ease of mobility throughout the flat with as few doors as is practical. A lobby or hall is a hindrance to movement and should be avoided. Recessing the entrance doorway restricts the sight-lines into the flat and helps to maintain privacy for the bed-sit flat off the public space. The bed-sitting room should accommodate the following: a bed with a minimum access width of 900 mm (36 in) either side, an easily accessible wardrobe, two chairs, a small dining table with chairs adjacent to a mini-kitchen and a reasonable amount of other furniture. The mini-kitchens should be part of the room, with good lighting. It should be equipped with a small sink and cooker comprising a small oven with two heating rings, a small refrigerator, and a worktop space with room for a toaster and electric kettle. Simple meals and beverages can be prepared by the resident if he or she feels able to, thus giving the opportunity for entertaining friends. The furnishing layout should be carefully considered to permit easy movement around the room. The television should be positioned so that it may be viewed from the bed.

The bathroom should be designed as an adaptable space with provision for the fixing of mobility aids to suit the resident. As with all bathrooms for the elderly, the door should open out. Some frail elderly may cope with a bath, others may prefer a hand-held shower with a seat positioned to suit their disability. The space and plumbing design should permit change from bath to shower and vice-versa. The warden alarm speech unit is best positioned by the bedhead, with an additional alarm pull in the bathroom. To provide the accommodation described a floor area of approximately 29 m² (312 sq ft) will be required. The plans of the Portsmouth project illustrate a typical bed-sit flat (Plan 2).

As previously emphasised, the operation of taps, window and door furniture, lavatory-roll holders and kitchen equipment must be easy for arthritic fingers.

Wardens' dwellings

Good wardens are essential to any sheltered scheme. The accommodation offered must therefore be of a high standard and planned to enable the warden to keep a discreet view of comings and goings while still enjoying a private life with his or

DETAILED DESIGN GUIDANCE

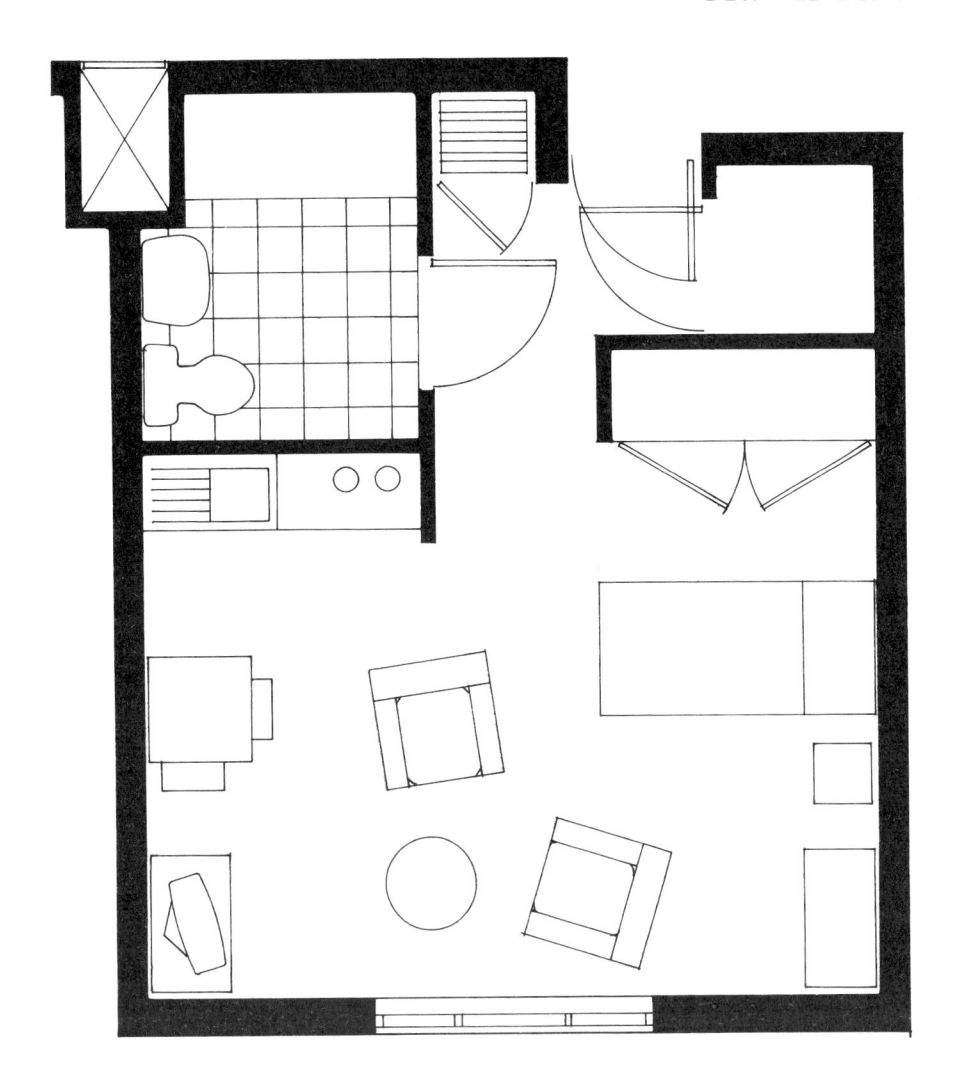

Plan 2   Bedsit flat

her family. Private access from outdoors is essential so that the warden and family may come and go without being waylaid by residents. Meetings with residents and peripatetic support personnel should take place in a separate office. The House Builders' Federation advice note on Sheltered Housing for Sale recommends that the warden's accommodation should be suitable for four or five persons. Offering a larger dwelling for the warden increases the overhead costs on a scheme but widens the range of suitable wardens. The larger unit will accommodate a family, encouraging a warden to start younger and stay longer. The following space standards are for a five-person dwelling:

Minimum overall size	Bungalow	80.0 m² (861 sq ft)
	Flat	82.5 m² (888 sq ft)
	Two-storey house	86.5 m² (931 sq ft)

Design notes   Provide a five-person dwelling with direct access to exterior.

Provide direct access from the warden's dwelling to the scheme, not off the common room but close to an office and the main entrance.

Provide a kitchen or living room window to overlook the main entrance and car park area.

Provide a private garden if possible.

61

DETAILED DESIGN GUIDANCE

Common areas

Entrance foyer

The entrance foyer to sheltered flats should be welcoming and easily identified from the access road. It should be entered by a level access, with a flush threshold protected by a canopy so that residents can search for keys without getting rained on (Figures 23 and 24). The foyer acts as an informal meeting place and should be large enough to provide a small sitting space off the main route, where people may wait. The sitting space can be usefully located near the office. Casual meetings in the foyer engender a sense of community and establish neighbourly contact without the residents having relationships thrust upon them. It is important therefore that the

Fig. 23 The main entrance should be welcoming and the design appropriate to the scale of the building. This entrance to Cherry Tree Court illustrates the main requirements of a ramped access with a flush threshold protected from rain by a canopy. The door is electronically locked. During certain hours it is unlocked for ease of use by tradesmen. The lock is master-keyed so that the residents' personal flat key will also operate the front door. Note the two-way speech unit by the door provided for visitors. (Architects: Francis Weal & Partners. Photo: Alan Williams)

Fig. 24   *Main entrance to Herbert Dane Court, Faversham. A level access protected from rain, well lit and with the front door electronically controlled. (Architects: Francis Weal & Partners. Photo: Robert Wilkinson)*

Fig. 25 *This double height common room at Daventry, with its sloping ceiling, is full of interest and encourages informal grouping of seats. The dining room in this scheme opens off the common room. Note the provision for coat hanging behind the fireplace wall. (Architects: Phippen Randall and Parkes)*

space should aid this social interchange, which can be enhanced if the foyer enjoys a good view and sunlight. The common room, office and main staircase should be easily identifiable from the foyer. The lift is best situated near the entrance, but screened from immediate view to discourage casual 'joy-riders'.

Design notes
Ensure the entrance is welcoming and easily identifiable.
Provide ramped access.
Provide space for informal meetings.
Locate common room, office and main stair off the foyer.
Ensure easy access to lift and residential part of the building.

Common room or lounge

In public-funded schemes there is a minimum size for common room facilities to be designed to, as follows:

Category 1 flats   0.9 m² (9.7 sq ft) per person
Category 2 flats   1.9 m² (20.5 sq ft) per person

A common room of 57 m² (614 sq ft) for 30 residents is large enough for most formal and informal uses. The space should be designed to permit congregate use for formal meetings, talks, slide shows, etc., and informal loose groups for coffee and conversation. Avoid the waiting-room syndrome: small bays off the main space invite more intimate groupings of tables and chairs. Consider the volume of the space: a raised ceiling will enhance the space (Figure 25). If the common room is within the volume of the main building and the ceiling cannot be raised consider using a recessed pot or ribbed structural floor over to help take light fittings up into recesses, thus avoiding an oppressive ceiling dotted with light fittings, smoke detectors, etc. (Figure 26). Careful choice of volume, colour and texture will ensure that a

Fig. 26 The common room will be used for formal and informal meetings. This example at Herbert Dane Court, Faversham, enjoys views over the adjoining road, giving residents whose flats may look on to the rear garden a change of view and the opportunity of seeing the street scene and feeling 'in touch'. Note the coffered ceiling which incorporates light fittings and smoke detectors, thus avoiding a cluttered and institutional appearance. (Architects: Francis Weal & Partners. Photo: Robert Wilkinson)

Fig. 27 Communal lounge and dining room. This example at Almere, Netherlands, designed by Herman Hertzberger, is part of the central hall of a large complex and is designed for multiple use.

DETAILED DESIGN GUIDANCE

common room receives multiple use (Figure 27). Too large a room may easily become a sea of tables and chairs with an oppressive ambience.

In schemes catering for more than thirty people, better use of additional common-room space can be found by creating additional common rooms, or informal meeting places, around the building. Common spaces may also be developed as hairdressing, hobbies or workshop rooms.

Common rooms of the size and type discussed are not appropriate to all schemes. Small Category 1 schemes operate successfully without a common room, the residents arranging meetings with management in their own homes. Any scheme of more than 20 units should be provided with a room for formal management meetings. The use or nature of the common room will change according to the residents' social activities and aspirations. The common room should be linked with a pantry for the preparation of light refreshments such as tea and coffee. The pantry should be no less than 5 m² (54 sq ft), and fitted with a sink and worktop, a refrigerator and cooker for preparing an occasional light meal. A space opening off or adjacent to the common room is essential for storing chairs not required for day-to-day use in the common room. This chair store should be not less than 2 m² (21.5 sq ft) and fitted with a shelf to stack table games – chess, backgammon, etc. In schemes where luncheon club meetings are envisaged, the chair store and pantry will need to be significantly larger.

The common room is a neutral meeting place. It provides the opportunity for residents to meet and also to enjoy a change of view. The room outlook should cater for this. Where most flats are looking 'inwards', the common room should 'look out' to the outside world; if most flats 'look out' then there is a strong case for a view on to internal landscaped gardens.

The common room should, in any event, open on to an outdoor sitting space. This outdoor space should be orientated to enjoy the sun and be suitably paved and laid out to facilitate small groups of seating, if possible screened from flats and other dwellings.

Design notes Floor space 57–75 m² (614–807 sq ft) (Category 2 Schemes).
Design for easy access from the entrance foyer.
Design the space for interesting multiple use.
Provide a pantry and chair store.
Orientate the room to give interesting views.
Open on to a private, sunny terrace.
Provide WC nearby.

Luncheon clubs

Provision is sometimes made in public sector schemes for luncheon clubs. These provide a midday cooked meal in the common room. Part of the common room may be furnished with tables and chairs, but additional tables and chairs are set out for lunch (Figure 28). For ease of operation, stacking chairs and tables must be housed in a convenient store with a minimum floor area of 4 m² (43 sq ft). For the preparation of lunch, a larger kitchen is required with a minimum floor area of 16 m² (172 sq ft). This area should include space for a dry store and deep freeze. The kitchen should serve the common room via a hatch and have easy access to and from the room. A direct, short access for goods into the kitchen, and refuse disposal, is important. There should be an entrance lobby for staff, with a lockable store for coats. The internal planning of the kitchen should allow for sequential storage, preparation, cooking and serving of lunch and subsequent collection and washing up. Cooking smells must be extracted and directed away from windows.

Design notes Design for flexible use with storage for stacking chairs and tables.
Provide a kitchen with easy access for goods and disposal of refuse.
Provide separate access for staff.
Provide extract ventilation to kitchen.
Provide WC nearby.

Fig. 28 The dining space for luncheon clubs can usefully be planned as an extension of the common room. This example at Palmer School Road, Wokingham, illustrates the possibilities of creating a light and airy space when it is situated outside the main volume of the building and the ceiling can be raised. (Architects: Phippen Randall and Parkes. Photo: Peter Cook)

DETAILED DESIGN GUIDANCE

Fig. 29   Shower Room. Equipped with a slotted bench seat, hinged to fold away when not required, with a vertical grab rail to hand. Note the shower head which is adjustable for height. The operating valve here is beneath the shower head; a better arrangement would be to have the valve by the grab rail so that the temperature of the water could be assessed prior to entering the shower area. (Photo: Alan Williams)

Communal WCs

Incontinence is one of the problems of the ageing process. It is important therefore to provide WC facilities near the common room and entrance foyer. They should not be entered from the common room or foyer. In small schemes a single WC may be acceptable; in any event a WC suitable for wheelchair use must be provided with drop-down grab rails either side of the WC. As in the case of bathrooms, the entry door must open out. A warden alarm call point should be provided clear of the door swing.

Design notes   Provide space for wheelchair use.
Provide grab rails and warden call point.
Entry door should open out.
Provide warden alarm call point.

Guest room

The guest room is an essential part of the scheme, especially where a high proportion of the dwellings is for single persons. The room is usually made available to residents' guests wishing to stop over for a night. In small schemes, where there is only one resident warden, the guest room provides accommodation for a relief warden. The location of the room is not important and it can be situated on any level. It is desirable to design the guest accommodation en suite with a shower and WC room approached via a lobby. The shower may then be used as a communal facility for residents unable to use a bath. The layout of the shower room should enable easy wheelchair access with space for changing. Avoid step-up shower trays: the floor should be water-tight and slope gently to a corner floor gully. A fixed slatted bench in the changing area in line with a hinged slatted bench seat in the shower area is of assistance to handicapped people (Figure 29). They may change, then slide over to the bench in the wet area and pull the shower curtain between the two benches. Hingeing the seat in the wet area enables them to use the shower without the seat if it is not required. The shower room is a place where accidents could occur: therefore a warden alarm

DETAILED DESIGN GUIDANCE

space for two single beds a table and two chairs.

jack socket for warden call master unit for use by temporary warden.

television ariel socket.

wardrobe   mini kitchen

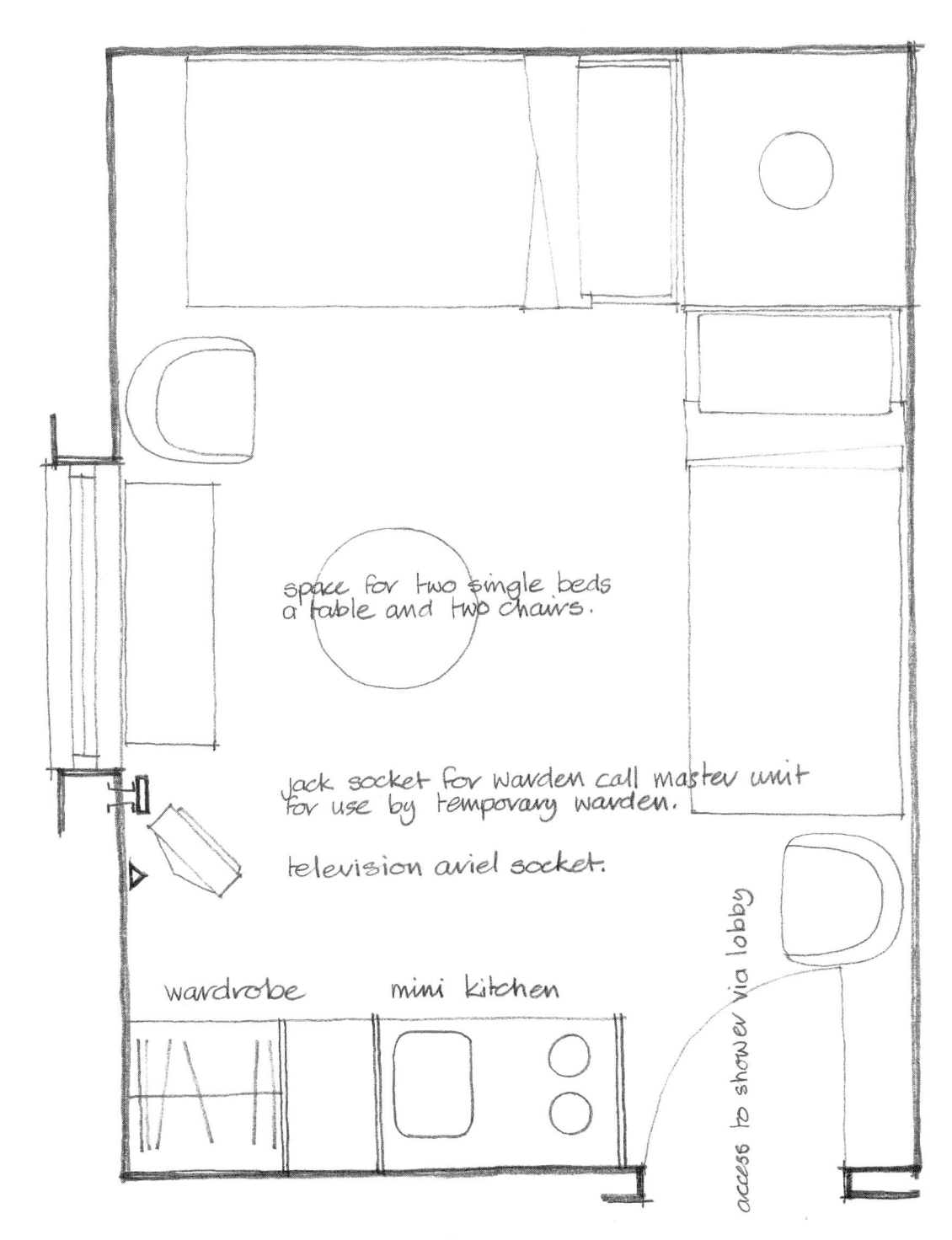

access to shower via lobby

The location, orientation and aspect of the guest room is not critical. It will be used mainly for visitors stopping overnight. On occasion it may house a temporary warden whilst the resident warden is away.

Fig. 30 Typical guest room

DETAILED DESIGN GUIDANCE

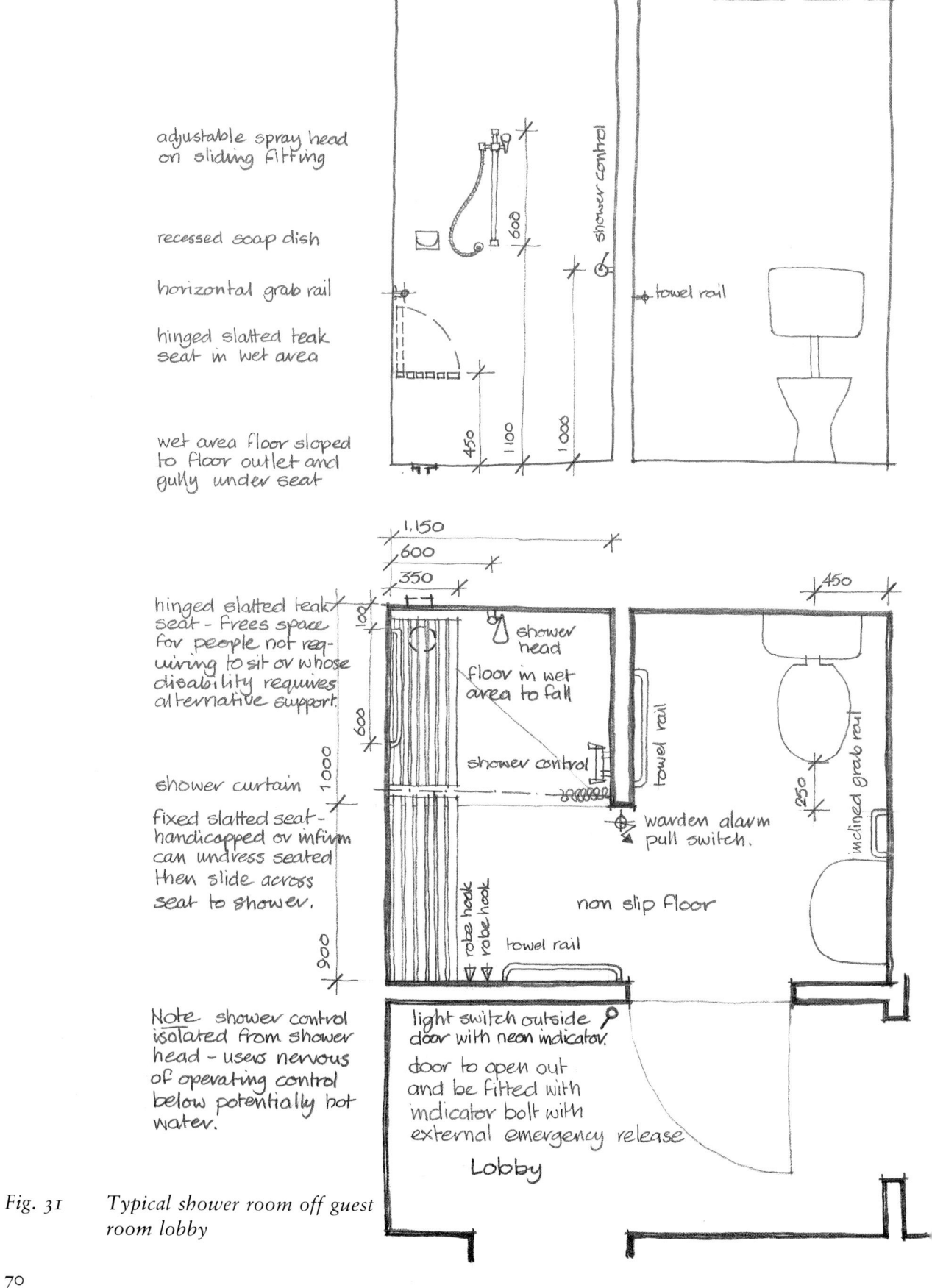

Fig. 31   Typical shower room off guest room lobby

DETAILED DESIGN GUIDANCE

pull is required. Figures 30 and 31 illustrate a typical guest room and shower layout.

The guest room should not be smaller than 13 m² (140 sq ft) with space for two single beds, two chairs, a wardrobe and a bedside table. As the room may be used by a relief warden, provision should be made for a mini-kitchen and space for television viewing. A suitable position should be designated for plugging in the warden alarm unit when required.

Design notes
Design en suite with shower room and mini-kitchen.
Minimum guest room area 13 m² (140 sq ft).
Provide warden alarm cord in shower.
Provide position for warden alarm unit.

Warden's office

The office should open off the entrance foyer and, where practical, should be close to the warden's dwelling. It will be used for general administration and meeting visitors. A minimum floor area of 6 m² (65 sq ft) is advisable to accommodate a desk, a chair, a visitor's chair and a filing cabinet. A telephone and warden call master unit should be grouped conveniently by the desk. The warden call unit should be positioned so as to be visible from the entrance foyer. This can be achieved by providing a glazed panel in the partition to the foyer. Any alarm being raised should be quickly noticed and the warden or other residents alerted. An external window should be provided to give a view of the entrance to the scheme.

Design notes
Minimum floor area 6 m² (65 sq ft).
Locate off entrance foyer with external views of the entrance.
Provide warden call master unit visible from the foyer.

Laundry

Where there is insufficient space within dwellings to install domestic laundry equipment, it is important to provide a communal laundry. The laundry is an essential part of all flat developments. Apart from its utilitarian value, it provides a social meeting place. It should be located at ground level adjacent to an outdoor drying area. Care should be taken to isolate structural and airborne sound, generated by machines, from the dwellings. The laundry should not share party walls with dwellings or be positioned under flats. When considering the route to the laundry avoid situations where residents have to pass through the entrance foyer. Residents tend to be self-conscious about trotting with their laundry baskets past areas where there may be visitors. A route from the lift away from the scheme entrance is best.

The size of the laundry will be determined by the number of residents to be served. As a general rule for schemes of about 30 units a laundry of about 12 m² (130 sq ft) is suitable. The proportions of the laundry will be determined by the layout of equipment. In practice the room should be at least 2.7 m (9 ft) wide. In large schemes of more than 60 flats with a high demand on laundry machines and drying space, it may be beneficial to provide two laundries. In schemes for the frail elderly where there is an element of nursing, a separate staff laundry will be necessary, fitted with a sluice for cleaning soiled sheets. This staff laundry should be near the extra-care flats.

The machines in the communal laundry should be simple to operate and should include a washing machine, a tumble drier (with vent through an external wall) and space for a spin drier. The isolating switches for these machines must be easily accessible (Figure 32). A sink unit will be required for soaking clothes and a worktop for folding clothes. Space should be provided for an ironing board. Storage should be available for mops, etc. to clean out the laundry. The floor should be waterproof and non-slip with a floor gully for draining away any overflows of water. Good ventilation should be provided, by mechanical extraction where appropriate. As the

DETAILED DESIGN GUIDANCE

Fig. 32 *Laundry. Simple-to-operate washing machine and tumble dryer. Note that the machine-isolating switch is not behind any equipment, thus providing easy access in an emergency. (Photo: Alan Williams)*

DETAILED DESIGN GUIDANCE

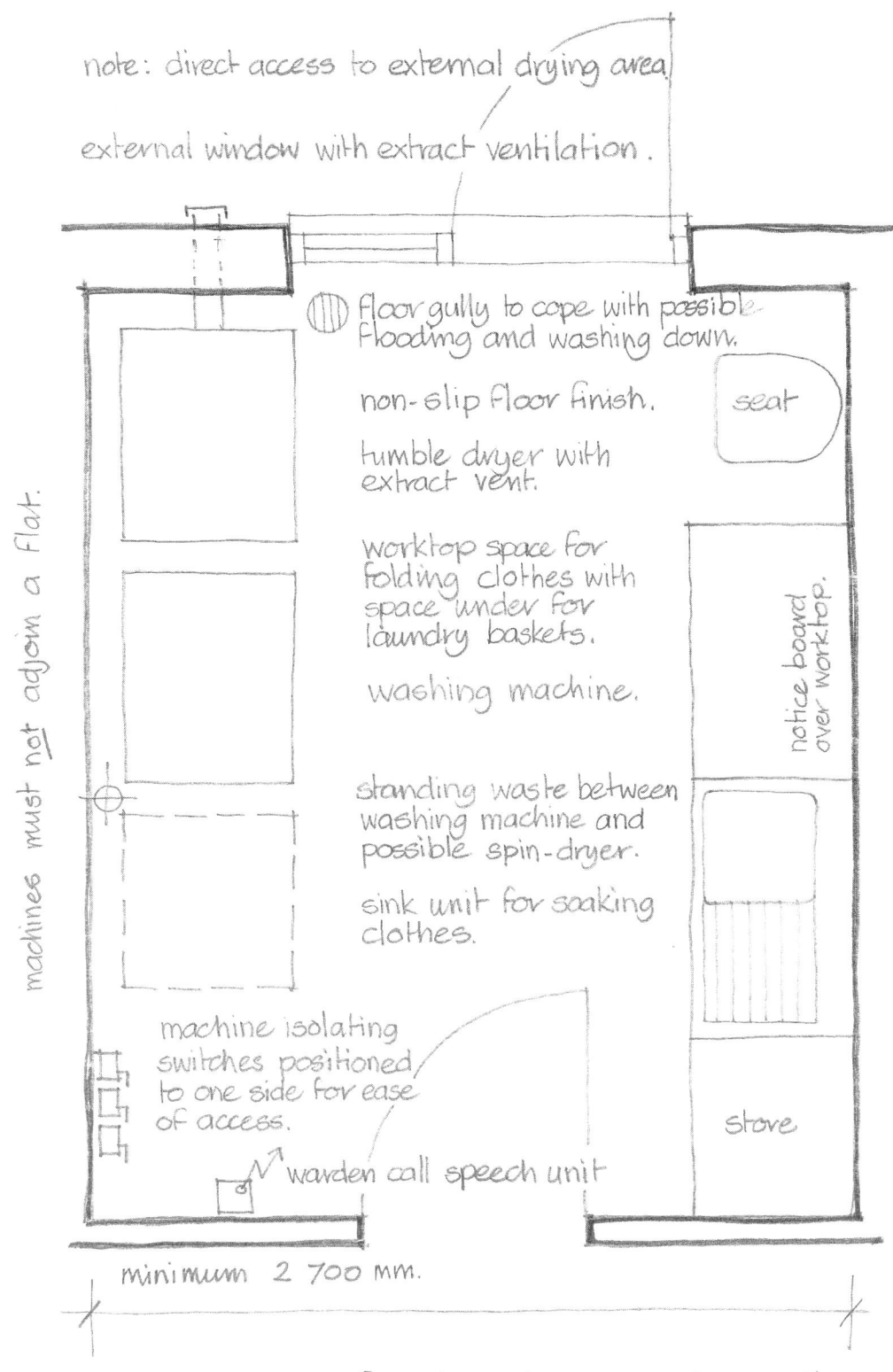

note: direct access to external drying area

external window with extract ventilation.

floor gully to cope with possible flooding and washing down.

non-slip floor finish.

tumble dryer with extract vent.

worktop space for folding clothes with space under for laundry baskets.

washing machine.

standing waste between washing machine and possible spin-dryer.

sink unit for soaking clothes.

machine isolating switches positioned to one side for ease of access.

warden call speech unit

seat

notice board over worktop.

stove

machines must not adjoin a flat.

minimum 2 700 mm.

for a typical scheme of 30 units a minimum floor area of 11 sq.m is advised.

Fig. 33   Typical laundry layout.

DETAILED DESIGN GUIDANCE

laundry is well used, it is a good place to locate a residents' notice board.

Figure 33 illustrates a typical laundry.

Design notes
Isolate laundry noise from dwellings.
The route to the laundry should not pass through the entrance foyer or the common room.
Provide easy access to external drying space.
Minimum floor area 12 m² (130 sq ft) – in large schemes consider separate laundries.
In frail elderly schemes provide a separate laundry with sluice facilities.

Telephone kiosk

In publicly funded schemes a telephone kiosk will be required for residents who may not have a private telephone. It is good practice however to provide conduit and draw wires throughout the scheme to enable private telephone installation as and when required.

The kiosk with its pay telephone is best located near the common room but away from flats, warden's dwelling or office. The entry door should open out and be partly glazed down to near floor level so that anyone collapsing in the kiosk can be quickly seen (Figure 35). Space for wheelchair users should be provided and the kiosk should be fitted with a shelf for note taking and directories, a bench seat and a notice board.

Design notes
Locate near common spaces but away from dwellings.
Fit out for wheelchair and ambulant users.
Provide partly glazed outward opening door.

Refuse disposal

At an early stage of the design process the local authority should be consulted on its method and times of refuse collection. Some authorities will use bulk storage collection vehicles for which mobile bulk storage containers must be provided

Fig. 34 Refuse store. Note the bulk refuse containers on wheels, and the ramped access and flush threshold. Refuse store doors must be sturdily constructed and fitted with robust hinges and hold-open devices. (Photo: Alan Williams)

(Figure 34). These containers (or 'paladins') may be purchased or in some cases rented from the local authority. For schemes of up to 30 units two paladins are sufficient. As a general rule refuse bin and paladin stores must be located within 15 m (50 ft) of the hard standing for the collection vehicle. Any incline from the store to the vehicle should slope down to the vehicle point. Where paladins are used the access formation should be a hard surface and not tarmac.

DETAILED DESIGN GUIDANCE

Fig. 35 *Telephone kiosk. The entry door opens out and is partly glazed, down to near floor level.*
(Photo: Alan Williams)

DETAILED DESIGN GUIDANCE

The best location for the bin store is on the north-facing aspect of the building. Avoid exposure to the sun, causing a heat build-up which will generate obnoxious smells. Where this is not practicable smells should be mechanically extracted and discharged at high level away from dwellings.

Having considered external access, the internal route from dwelling to store should be carefully planned to reduce carrying distance and inconvenience. Preferably the store should be near the lift, with the entrance away from any flat and from the common room. Access should be through a well ventilated lobby.

The method of refuse collection from the dwellings should be determined early on in the design stage. In some schemes residents will carry their own mini-plastic sacks to the main store; an alternative is to provide collection points at each floor level adjacent to the lift. These collection points should have well ventilated lobby access, and the store should also be well ventilated with fly screens. Wall-mounted frames should be provided for large refuse sacks, which will be collected and transferred to the main refuse store.

Generally the main store should not be less than 10 m² (108 sq ft). A floor gulley with an external tap will be necessary for washing out the store. Where paladins are used a raised platform will enable easy transference of sacks into the bulk storage container. Refuse stores and their access doors get hard usage, so the external door should be strongly made, with heavy-duty hinges and a stout hold-open catch. The door reveals will need protection, and a substantial timber buffer 400 mm (16 in) above floor level will protect the internal walls from damage.

Design notes
External access within 15 m (50 ft) of collection vehicle hard standing.
Internal access via ventilated lobby close to lift.
Determine method of refuse collection.
Provide facilities for washing down the store.
Avoid nuisance of smells.
Construct external access robustly.

Cleaners' storage

In small schemes the cleaner's store can be incorporated into the laundry. Generally a store of approximately 2 m² (22 sq ft) will be required at each floor level to accommodate an industrial-type vacuum cleaner and a bucket sink. Shelving for cleaning materials should be provided. The store is most conveniently located near the lift.

Design notes
Provide a store on all upper floors.
Fit out with bucket sink, shelves and coat hooks.

Boiler house

Where a central boiler house is required – and this applies to most publicly funded schemes – it should be located so as to provide the most economic distribution of pipes and to avoid nuisance to residents. The noise generated by boilers will be borne by the structure to adjacent rooms: isolating the slab and distribution pipes will help prevent this structurally borne sound, but the best practice is to isolate the boiler room entirely. The boiler room can be located successfully at first-floor level over the refuse room, provided the design takes into account future service access and renewal of boilers. When using gas as fuel a gas intake room should be provided at ground-floor level, adjacent to or below the boiler room. The gas intake room should have direct external access and natural ventilation.

The size of the boiler room will be determined by the size and layout of the heating plant. The layout should enable easy access for maintenance and for reaching controls. As a general rule, for schemes of about 30 units, 20 m² (215 sq ft) of floor space will be required. A floor gulley should be provided to facilitate washing down and draining of the system.

Design notes
Locate to provide economic pipe distribution.
Isolate from flats.
Plan for boiler maintenance and renewal.

Tank room

The most economic position for the tank room is over the boiler room. The area required will be determined by the storage requirement of the local water authority. The room should be planned for easy access via a telescopic loft ladder, with sufficient space around and above the tanks for servicing.

Design notes
Locate over boiler room.
Determine local water authority storage requirement.
Provide easy access for service.

Electrical switchroom

One of the determining factors in the location of the switchroom is the route of the incoming main and the distribution routes within the building. In schemes providing a lift a three-phase supply will be required to the lift machine or pump room. The switchroom is best planned on the ground floor, although its location is not critical as long as it provides reasonable access internally for re-setting time clocks and controls. For most schemes a space of about 7 m² (75 sq ft) will be required, with one wall at least 3 m (10 ft) in length to accommodate the intake, meters and distribution boards. Residents' consumer units should be positioned by the flat entrances.

Design notes
Consider external main and internal service routes.
Provide internal access for re-setting controls.

Battery room

Emergency lighting for escape routes can be provided by self-contained units or battery-supplied units. Where battery-supplied units are to be used a battery room of about 3 m² (32 sq ft) should be planned, with internal access and external ventilation.

Design notes
Determine method of power supply to emergency light fittings.

Communal facilities: frail elderly schemes

All the requirements for a Category 2 scheme will be found in frail elderly schemes. Accommodation for extra staff, both resident and peripatetic, will be required. As 24-hour cover will be necessary, the scheme should accommodate a relief warden and a base for overnight nursing staff.

Residents will take their main meals in a dining room, so full catering facilities must be planned in the kitchen, which should be located by the service access. Dining space may be designed centrally or it may be dispersed, providing smaller and more intimate spaces closer to the residents' flats with meals distributed by trolley. A small domestic-size laundry would be beneficial for those residents competent to do their own washing, though most would be done by staff in a fully-equipped laundry. It must be assumed, too, that many residents will not be able to bath or shower unassisted, so an assisted bathroom should be provided on each floor.

Contact with the outside world will be primarily visual, as mobility is impaired and journeys through the complex are much more difficult for frail than for 'active' elderly. It follows that all flats should have an interesting and outward-looking view, as far as is consistent with the need for a sense of security. The latter is best achieved by having a private zone of space between the dwelling windows and the boundary; the latter should be secure and defined by railings. The route through the building must be clear and simple to avoid confusion. Corridors without external views induce disorientation. Vertical circulation will in most cases be by lift, so additional lifts may be required. Access to staircases is of secondary importance and will be determined largely by the fire brigade's requirements for fire-fighting: as a means of escape they are dangerous. We consider it better to isolate the source of fire and keep the residents in their rooms to save accidents from falls. Single-banked flats with well-glazed routes to one side also enable staff and other residents to keep a discreet eye on people moving throughout the building. Sitting areas off the circulation route should have a WC nearby.

Design notes
Plan additional staff accommodation.
Provide kitchen/dining facilities.
Provide assisted bathrooms on each floor.
Ensure residents' sense of security.
Ensure site's security.

Routes through the building should be simple, well lit, and open one side where possible.
Provide additional lifts for vertical circulation.
Provide WCs by sitting areas.

DETAILED DESIGN GUIDANCE

Fig. 36 Corridor: Palmer School Road, Wokingham. This carefully detailed example of good corridor design illustrates the main features that are desirable in internal routes. It is interesting and well lit, with views out, recessed flat entrance doorways and ample opportunities for residents to 'colonise' the space with plants. For reasons of smoke containment doorways are planned at strategic points in the route. By using electronically controlled magnetic door holders, the doors can be held open during daylight hours. Activation of smoke detectors automatically causes the doors to close, thus containing smoke. (Architects: Phippen Randall and Parkes. Photo: Jo Reid and John Peck)

Fig. 37 End of corridor: Cherry Tree Court, Harwell. The top part of the louvred window is automatically controlled by smoke detectors; the bottom part is manually operated. The British Standard Code of Practice requires that where smoke dispersal methods are used to facilitate escape, ventilators should have a free opening area of not less than 1.5 m² (approximately 15 sq ft) of which 0.5 m² (approximately 5 sq ft) should be either permanently open or automatically controlled by smoke detectors; the remaining area may be manually or automatically controlled. (Architects: Francis Weal & Partners. Photo: Alan Williams)

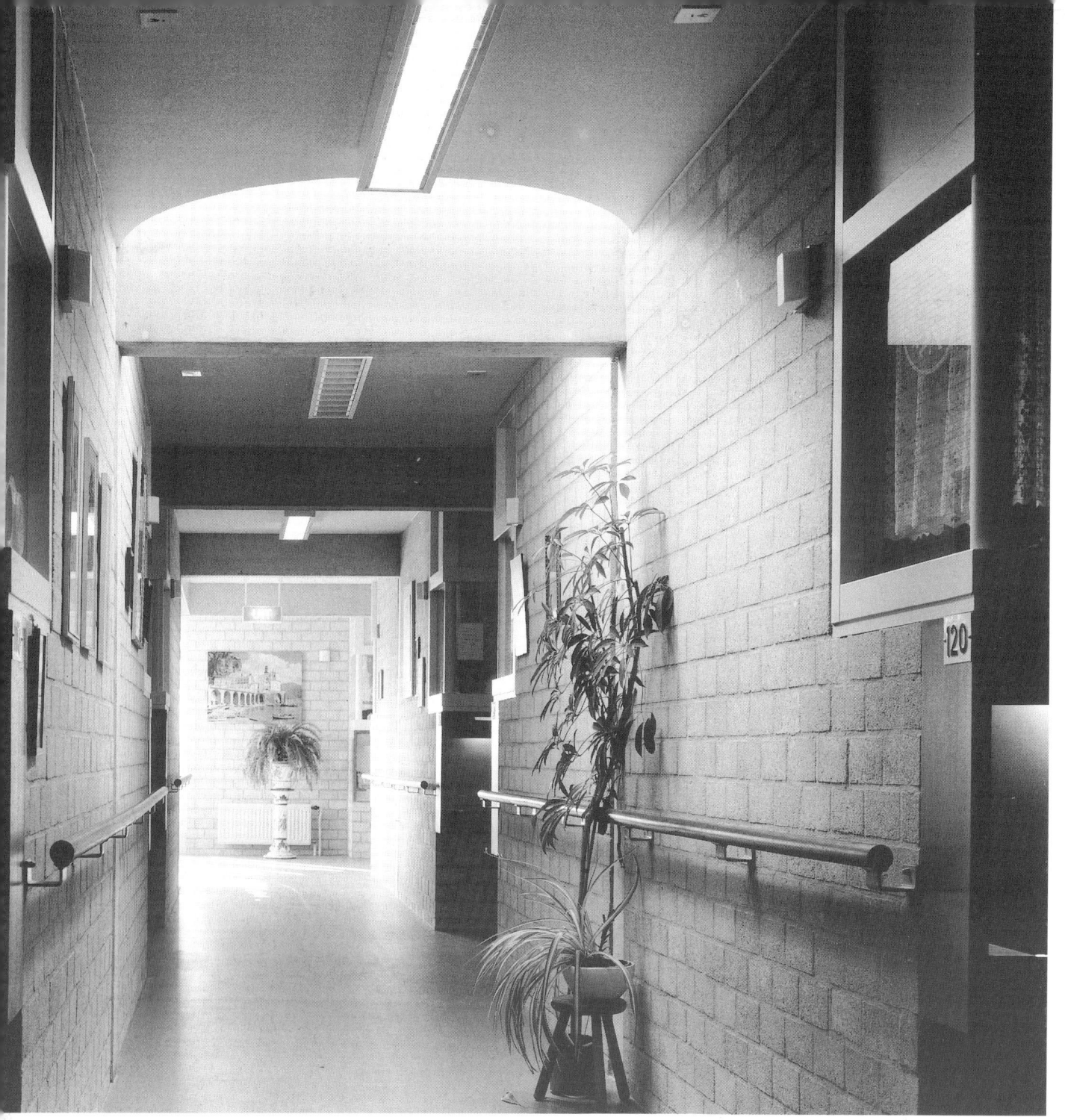

Figs. 38 and 39 Corridors: De Overloop, Almere Haven, Netherlands. The corridors in this scheme are good examples of interesting routes through a building. The detailed design invites, and allows, the residents to personalise the areas by their flats. Note the kitchen windows looking on to the corridor and the delivery hatches by the flat entrance doors. Handrails in the corridor are provided to assist mobility. (Architect: Herman Hertzberger. Photo: Martin Charles)

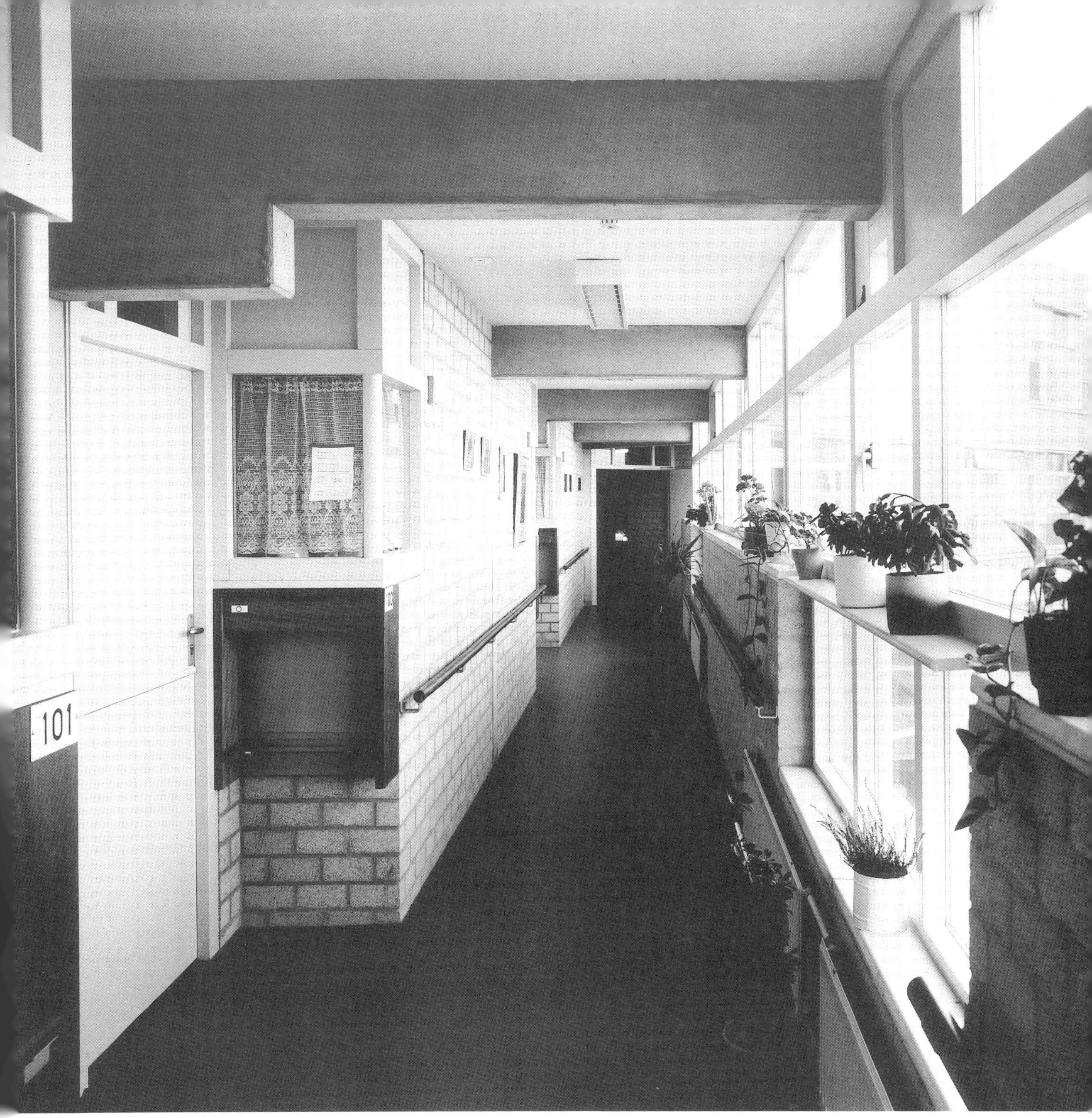
101

DETAILED DESIGN GUIDANCE

Corridors and staircases

The point was made in Chapter 2 that access routes throughout the scheme should be interesting, with natural lighting wherever possible and opportunities created beside the entrance doors of flats and at the ends of corridors for decoration with plants (Figures 36–9). Steps must never be introduced into corridors: if changes in level are unavoidable then well-lit ramps may be used instead (though it must be remembered that ramps are not really suitable for the frail elderly using walking frames). For general circulation the minimum corridor width is 1200 mm (48 in). By lifts and other common areas where people may congregate the corridor width must be increased, particularly where doors open on to the corridor, as in the case of communal WCs. It is common practice in Category 2 schemes, and essential in frail elderly schemes, to provide a handrail along one wall of the corridor 915 mm (36 in) above floor level. Corridor floors should be carpeted to reduce impact noise. The use of differently coloured carpets and wall decoration for each storey helps residents to identify which floor they are on (e.g. the blue/green/yellow floor).

Staircases should be easy to climb, without long flights of steps. The rise of steps should not exceed 167 mm (6.6 in) and the tread or going should not be less than 290 mm (11.4 in). The stairway must have a minimum unobstructed width (between handrails) of 900 mm (36 in). The maximum recommended unobstructed width is 1100 mm (43.3 in). Handrails should be fitted on both sides of stair flights. The stairway should enjoy natural light and ventilation; where window ventilation gear is difficult to reach then remote control gear must be provided. Principal staircases should be carpeted with non-slip nosings clearly identifying the treads (Figures 40 and 41).

Figs. 40 and 41   Staircase: Cherry Tree Court, Harwell. Easy to climb, with handrails which are simple to grip. Note the non-slip nosings which are a different colour from the stair carpet so that the steps can be easily seen. (Architects: Francis Weal & Partners. Photo: Alan Williams)

DETAILED DESIGN GUIDANCE

5 LANDSCAPE

Judging by the wealth of publications on gardening, this civilized recreation is enjoyed by many people. Too often, however, housing for the elderly is set in a landscape 'designed' for passive recreation, institutional in character, merely a setting for the building. Lawns, trees and shrubs, arranged around hard surfaces required for access, car parking and sitting-out spaces, take on a corporate image which is at odds with the variety of personalities and talents being housed. They do not invite participation in the horticultural year by the residents, and thereby deny the full enjoyment of the garden. For many the move into sheltered housing has in part been prompted by worries about the maintenance of the old home and garden. However, it does not follow that they have lost interest in gardening. They may no longer be able to cut the grass or weed the herbaceous border, but they retain the skills of rooting plant cuttings and raising plants from seed. The community of elderly is a reservoir of stored knowledge which, given the right stimulus, can make a contribution to the neighbourhood. Given a herb garden or fruiting malus trees, Granny or Grandfather can pass on many culinary skills for which the ingredients of parsley, sage, rosemary, thyme, or crab apple jelly are important. The external landscape provides many opportunities for involving the residents in activities beneficial to residents and the local community.

In his paper 'Meeting client and user needs'[1] Tony Bubbage discusses the therapeutic nature of gardening for the elderly and the opportunities for involving other communities. He records a successful arrangement in which the children from a local school assisted with the weeding and visited the rabbits kept by the residents of a sheltered housing scheme, thus opening up a dialogue between school and residents.

Interest in the landscaped garden can also be heightened by the creation of a 'wild' garden to provide a habitat for flora and fauna. In a recent scheme[2] the architects have retained a natural pool and defined an area of land away from the main building to be managed as a 'wild' garden. An adjacent terrace enables the residents to sit and observe the birds and butterflies, and residents in flats overlooking the garden daily report sightings of animals and birds.

In all landscape schemes future maintenance costs must be considered. 'Wild' gardens do not necessarily mean low costs. The garden will still need management to prevent climax vegetation such as scrub and trees taking over. The landscape should be designed to make the most of natural features and structured to allow communal maintenance by contractors on the public side of the scheme and opportunities for the residents to cultivate smaller spaces in the private garden.

Having outlined opportunities for enhancing the quality of life in the scheme, we will now look at the elements forming the external landscape.

The overall objectives in the design of the external landscape may be stated as follows:

---

[1] Published in *Gardens and Grounds for Disabled and Elderly People*, proceedings of a seminar held by the Centre on Environment for the Handicapped, CEH, 1981

[2] Cherry Tree Court, Harwell. Francis Weal and Partners, 1986

LANDSCAPE

1. *To tailor the scheme to its environment.*
   This is a contextual problem, relating to scale and colour. The interaction between the landscape and the building should be complementary in scale and colour, making full use of natural features, mature trees, gradients, water, etc. to give an established character to the development by the time the residents move in. If it can be demonstrated at an early stage that someone cares about the landscape the garden is more likely to be cared for and enriched by the residents' horticultural skills, assuming scope is provided for them.

2. *Organisation of the space about the building for:*
   Vehicular and pedestrian approach.
   Public and private space.
   Residents' communal outdoor space.
   Residents' private outdoor space.
   Recreation outdoors.

Vehicular and pedestrian approach

The approach to the main entrance should be inviting. Wherever possible it should enable pedestrians to enter the building without crossing vehicular routes. In smaller schemes this may not be feasible, in which case the road should be surfaced with materials indicative of joint vehicular/pedestrian use, for instance brick or concrete block paviours (Figure 42).

Fig. 42 *Vehicular and pedestrian approach: Cherry Tree Court, Harwell. Pedestrians should not cross vehicular routes, but where it is impractical to plan the routes separately the footway and road should be surfaced with materials indicative of joint use. In this example concrete block paviours have been used. (Architects: Francis Weal & Partners. Photo Alan Williams)*

LANDSCAPE

A setting-down/picking-up point for visitors arriving by car or residents being collected should be situated close to the entrance. A dropped kerb at this point will facilitate access for wheelchair users transferring from cars.

Visitors' and residents' car parking in urban areas is best screened from view to minimise unauthorised parking – a source of irritation to residents. Car parks can be successfully screened with mounds of soil and planting. Bays should be clearly defined and generous manoeuvring zones provided.

Pedestrian routes should be clearly identified and designed to discourage intrusion. Care must be taken to ensure security. The space between the footpaths and the residents' dwellings should not invite intrusion. Shrub planting and railings can be used to deter casual intrusion and help reinforce a sense of security. For flatted developments external doors opening into the public side of the building should be kept to a minimum, preferably to only the main entrance. Escape doors from the building are best located opening on to the private or 'secure' side of the building.

For service deliveries and refuse collections the size of vehicles envisaged must be taken into account and suitable turning/reversing circles provided. Consultation with the authorities responsible for refuse collections will determine the mode and frequency of collection. Where bulk refuse containers are employed the pick-up point should be within 15m (50 feet) of the refuse store; any gradient must be less than 1:15 with the slope rising to the store to facilitate easy transfer of containers. As the containers run on small wheels the pathway surface must be capable of withstanding the wheel impact loading and must be easily negotiable.

Public and private space

The frontage of the scheme presents the 'public' landscape onto which the common rooms and the warden's office and flat should look out, to promote interest for the residents on the one hand and discreet control on the other. This zone of 'defensible' space should be laid out to avoid potential areas of concealment. For schemes without a warden, security can be reinforced by enabling windows from the residents' dwelling to overlook the space. The kitchen window is a convenient one for watching people come and go. Security fencing should be provided between the 'public' landscape and the residents' private garden in urban areas where there is a history of crime and vandalism.

Residents' communal outdoor space

For the enjoyment of the garden, terraces, footpaths and seating will be required. Access should be provided from the common room on to a terrace which should be orientated to obtain sunshine and shelter from winds. Sitting-out spaces in the garden should be screened by planting or walls to enable residents to enjoy the outdoors without the feeling of being overlooked by other residents or any adjoining development. (See Figures 43–5.)

Footpaths generally should be designed to permit people, some of whom may be handicapped and only able to use a wheelchair or frame, to pass easily. All changes in level should be carefully

Figs. 43, 44 and 45 *The garden: Homeleigh Court, London SW11. In a tightly planned urban area, the architects have created an outdoor space full of interest. The pergola and raised flower beds provide screened sitting out spaces. Note the use of low-level bulkhead fittings to light the footpath. (Architects: Phippen Randall and Parkes. Photo: Crispin Boyle)*

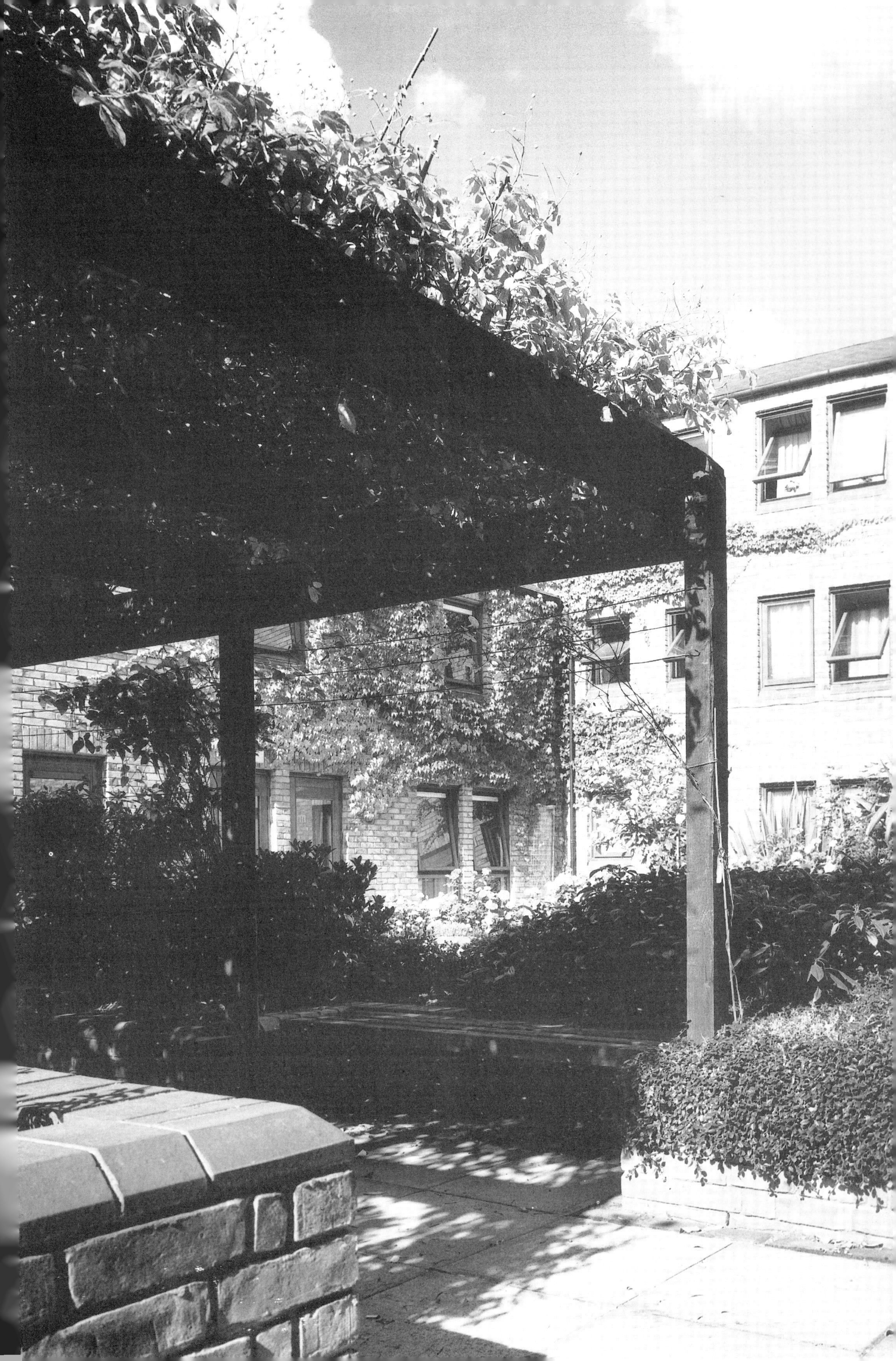

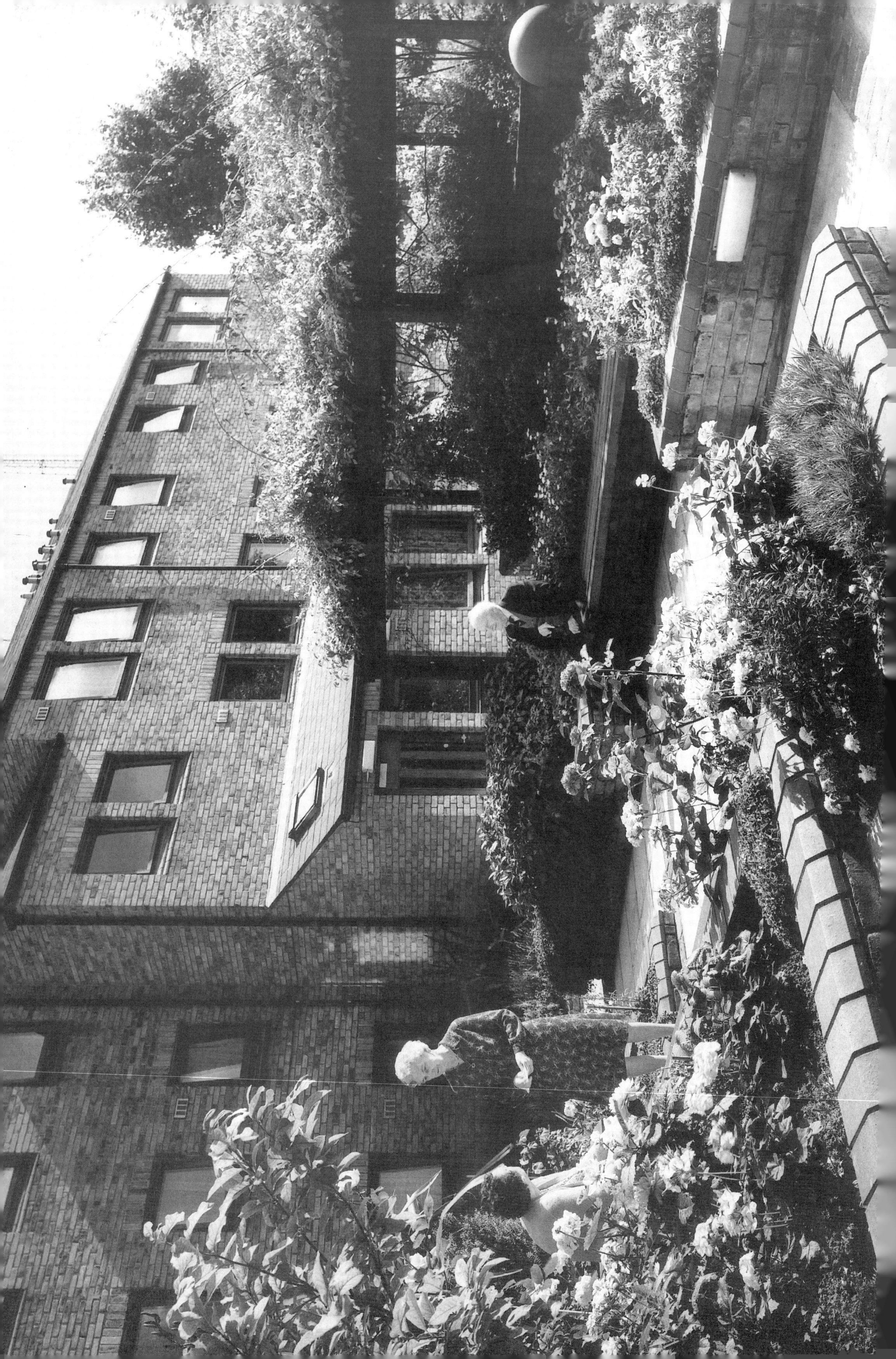

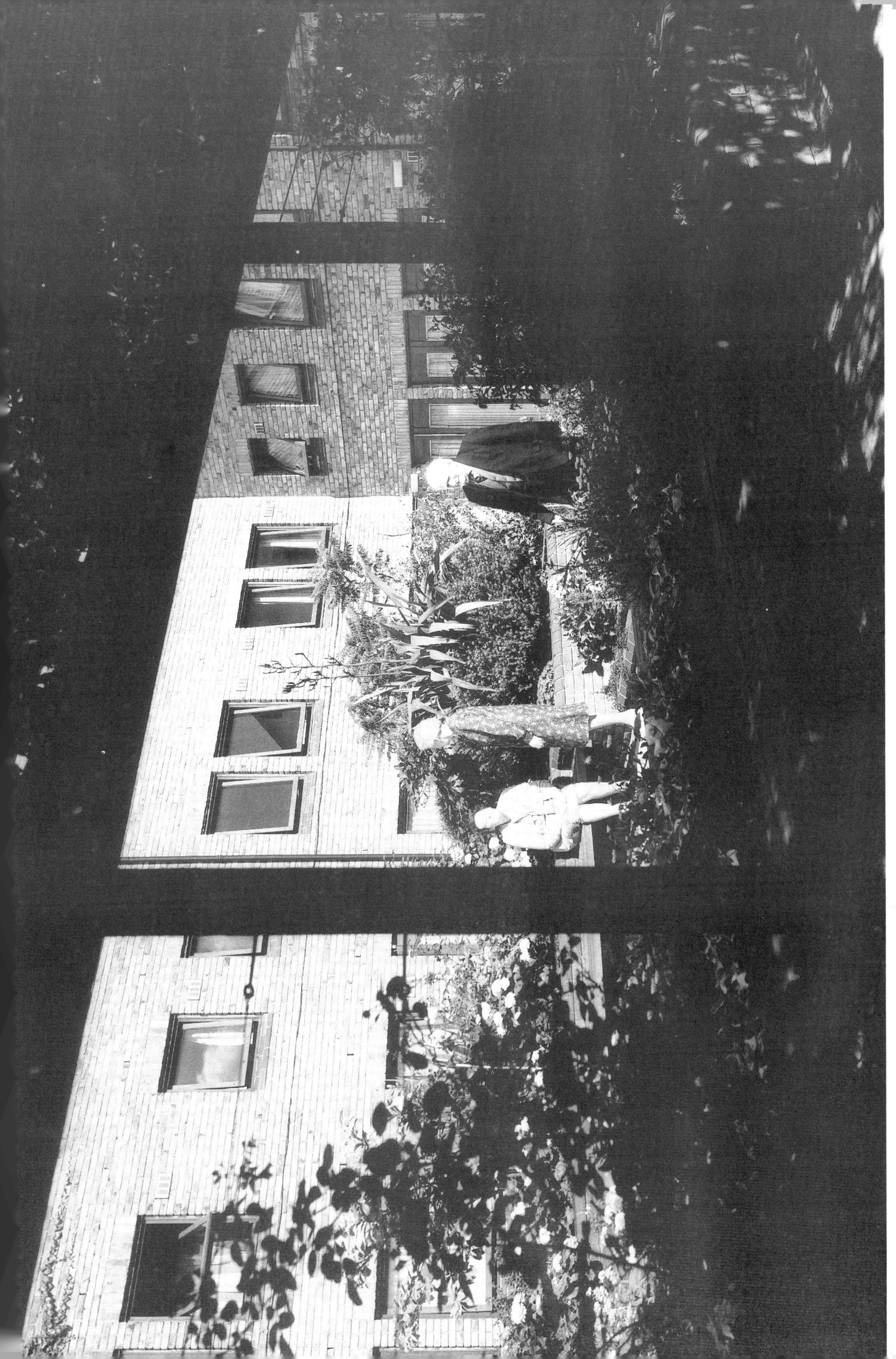

considered. Whilst access to doorways from the outside should generally be ramped (maximum slope 1:12) and steps avoided, long ramps can be a source of danger for anyone using a walking frame. Descending a ramp when using a frame, the centre of gravity is thrown forward, increasing the danger of a fall. Where long ramps are unavoidable, consideration should be given to an easily negotiable stepped ramp with a gentler slope and changes in level clearly identified.

Adjacent to the laundry, and screened from view, a drying area should be designated to accommodate one or two rotary clothes driers.

Residents' private outdoor space

Ground floor dwellings opening on to the private garden can enjoy a private sitting-out space, with small areas defined for cultivation by the residents. Simple timber screens between the dwellings provide a sense of place and sheltered corners for growing plants. Within the garden secluded outdoor sitting spaces, screened by plants, trellis or raised beds, can be provided so that residents from upper floors may also enjoy the garden and fresh air.

Recreation outdoors

Opportunities for outdoor recreation and gardening should be provided for residents. Raised planting beds and frames for plants to climb on will enable them to exercise their horticultural skills. These beds and frames may provide screening for the sitting-out places. For the full enjoyment of gardening, a greenhouse, with raised staging and a water supply, can be the source of much pleasure, enabling residents to raise plants for indoor or outdoor use. Alternatively, a conservatory can give the right climatic conditions for raising plants and seeds, with the added benefit of space for sitting in to enjoy the sunshine while being protected from cold winds. Finally, provision must be made on site for the storage of gardening tools and hose reels and an external water supply.

Elements in the landscape

Hard landscape

The designer can select from a wide range of surface materials. For pedestrian trafficked areas the prime consideration must be safety. Uneven, loose or slippery surfaces on which the elderly might trip or slide over must be avoided. The base for paved areas in particular must be well formed and consolidated to prevent uneven settlement of paviors. Different textures and colours can help define areas and ramps. Where changes of level occur, handrails help signpost the change and give assistance to the infirm.

Lighting

External lighting should provide the following:

1. Illumination of access routes.
2. Security lighting.
3. Creative lighting.

The space between the public street lighting and the entrance to the dwellings should have a scheme of lighting designed to provide a well lit footpath and car parking area. The lighting of access routes should define the way to the main entrance clearly.

All entrances to and escape routes from the building should be illuminated to ensure security from criminal loitering and avoid leaving areas in shade.

The creative use of illumination to highlight features in the landscape, or communal parts of the building, will enrich the night-time environment. Care must be taken to ensure that the lighting scheme does not become a source of irritation to residents through lights shining into flats.

External signs

Signs throughout the scheme should be kept to a minimum. With a well-organised design, routes should be obvious and residents will soon know the way about their new home. A multiplicity of signs creates an institutional feel which should be avoided at all costs. Signing of the building should be sufficient to identify the scheme for the casual visitor. The main entrance should be made obvious with the street sign well illuminated.

External seating

External seating for residents in the private garden, screened from overlooking, provides opportunities for quiet enjoyment of the outdoor space. Seating by access routes at the front of the building can lead to unwarranted use by non-residents or the irritation often felt by some residents at others 'clocking them in and out' of the scheme. Privacy must be respected within the communal concept.

The organic landscape

Organic landscaping is a specialist skill and the suitability of plants for any scheme will depend on a number of factors, including the pH of the soil (a measure of its acidity/alkalinity), orientation, exposure, plant compatibility and growth rates.

The management and maintenance policy for the landscape must be determined at the outset, as this will influence plant selection and landscape design. Designs employing ground cover and shrubs of slow growth will be cheaper to maintain. The use of plants requiring annual pruning or frequent replacement will increase maintenance costs. Raised beds, so advantageous for the elderly, will require additional watering and feeding as they can dry out so quickly in hot summers. However, if the opportunity is provided, residents may adopt parts of the garden to cultivate themselves. A wide range of gardening tools have been developed to enable the infirm and handicapped to carry out gardening tasks previously beyond the ability of many. Raised planting beds make cultivation possible for the ambulant infirm who can sit on the side of a raised planter to plant, weed and prune.

Plants attracting birds, bees and butterflies extend the scope of interest and enjoyment in the garden. Informal hedges can provide a habitat for nesting, and the flowers and fruits of some species invite visits from birds and bees. Colour, scale and texture should be carefully considered in the landscape design. Evergreens contribute to the garden structure, giving continuity, while deciduous plants provide changes of form and colour as the seasons pass. Strategic siting of scented plants by entrances or sitting-out areas will give pleasure to visitors and residents. A well-stocked herb garden can be a source of great interest if residents have knowledge to pass on of herb usage in cooking and homeopathic use.

6 | MEANS OF ESCAPE, FIRE PRECAUTIONS, SERVICES AND COMMUNICATIONS

Means of escape

In the design of any scheme the safety of residents in the event of fire must be carefully considered. In the simplest dwelling this may mean taking care that possible sources of fire, for instance the kitchen, can be isolated by a self-closing door to permit the escape of residents from habitable rooms. In flat development the decision has to be taken as to whether to design on a smoke dispersal or a smoke containment basis. Advice should be sought from the fire brigade serving the area on which procedure to adopt, as the brigades' requirements vary from area to area. The British Standard Code of Practice relating to precautions against fire and means of escape for Flats and Maisonettes[1] sets out the parameters for design, using dispersal or containment systems. Adoption of this code will satisfy the Building Regulations but not necessarily the fire brigade: you have been warned!

With smoke dispersal designs, doors across corridors are not required. But the escape stairs must be contained by fire-resisting doors. It is recognised that in most fires it is smoke which causes the majority of casualties. The smoke dispersal approach to the problem endeavours to clear the escape routes of smoke by means of automatic opening vents or windows at strategic positions operated by smoke detectors and heat sensors. There is some doubt about the efficiency of this system when no wind or air movement are available to clear the smoke. By maintaining a positive air pressure in the escape routes through mechanical pressurisation this problem may be overcome.

Smoke containment requires the introduction of fire doors across corridors, and that no flats be situated at the 'dead-end' of a corridor. For the elderly, negotiating fire doors in a corridor is a problem that can in itself cause accidents. Fire brigades will permit corridor fire doors (not the stair doors) to be kept open most of the day by electro-magnetic catches which release and close the door when fire or smoke is detected on a sensor. With the use of fire-resistant structures and non-inflammable finishes in escape routes it is difficult to support the containment theory, which places so many obstacles in the way of the elderly. For the frail elderly, most of whom would not endeavour to use the stairs, it is even more unlikely that containment would save casualties, caused either by fire or in the very process of evacuation.

Evacuation of a building occupied by the elderly is fraught with problems, to which there are no final answers. It is possible that in time thinking on this subject will change, permitting or indeed encouraging the elderly to stay put in the event of fire, and simultaneously containing the fire at its source.

Fire-fighting and alarm equipment

The fire brigade will advise on fire-fighting equipment. The first line of defence should be

[1] BSI, *British Standard Code of Practice: CP3*, Chapter IV, Part 1, 1971

simple lightweight equipment that the residents can use themselves, for instance fire blankets fitted in the kitchen. Heavy equipment and hose reels will not be usable by the elderly. Access for fire fighting equipment must be discussed with the fire brigade who will consider the proximity of fire hydrants and access for fire tenders and hose reels. Long corridors may require dry risers to be installed.

All flats should be protected by a fire alarm system operated by manual and automatic sensors. The fire brigade will advise on the provision of smoke and heat detectors and the location of manual fire alarm points. The alarm panel, with a visual display locating the zone of the fire, should be positioned by the warden's office, easily visible to people in the vicinity of the entrance.

The sound level required at the bedhead of sleeping persons is 75 decibels and the only practical way of achieving this is to install an alarm bell or sounder within the entrance hall of each flat. In addition to this, the warden call system can be connected via a relay to the fire alarm system so that upon activation of the fire alarms a warble tone can be transmitted over each speech unit. This item may only be classed as an additional warning. However, it cannot be considered as part of the official fire warning system as it derives its power from a separate source, and will be a different sound from the general alarm and one which is not acceptable under the Code of Practice relating to fire alarms.

Power for the fire alarm system will come from a separate 240 volt supply at the intake position, via a battery and charger unit which must be exclusive to the fire alarm system.

In the first few weeks of handing over a scheme, smoke detectors can be a source of great inconvenience and unnecessary alarm, actuating alarms without smoke being present. The detectors are very sensitive and unless they are kept dust free (by using plastic bags and tape) until *after* corridors and flat lobbies have been thoroughly cleaned, they can cause many false alarms. Vacuum cleaning of new corridor carpets raises considerable dust.

Services

In this section we consider mechanical, electrical and other services as follows:

1. Heating and Cooking
2. Water supply
3. Lighting
4. Lifts
5. Ventilation

1. Heating and cooking

Each winter the press reports alarming death rates of old people as a result of 'hypothermia'. However, studies of death rates among sample groups suggest that there is no clear-cut distinction between sample groups in well-heated environments and other groups in poorly-heated accommodation. The increased winter death rate arises from exposure, waiting around outdoors for buses or shopping when the lowered body heat results in heart failure. But most elderly people appreciate and expect a warm, comfortable environment free from draughts.

A decision must be made, early in the design process, on whether to instal a centralised system and defray the running costs of supplying heat and hot water by a service charge, or to provide individual heating units under the residents' own control. In public housing the centralised system is favoured. It has the advantage that heat under the control of a warden will ensure that no resident attempts to economise by switching off the heat source and so suffers the ill-effects of poor heating. In the private sector individual heating plants are favoured. Most people moving into retirement housing arc used to having the heat source under their own control and will be able to operate and budget for the energy consumed.

As many will be retiring on a fixed income, the future running costs of the heating system are of considerable importance. Walls, floors and ceiling must be insulated to a high standard and wherever possible windows double-glazed to keep running costs down. Cold bridges in the structure, causing condensation, should be avoided. The heat source

MEANS OF ESCAPE, FIRE PRECAUTIONS, SERVICES AND COMMUNICATIONS

controls, on individual systems, must be simple to understand and easy to use. With centralised systems provision should be made for a standby boiler to cover possible breakdowns.

A decision on the energy source must also be made at an early stage, the practical options being:

Gas
Oil
Electricity

Gas is favoured for most developments. There are no problems with fuel storage or delivery and it is reasonably economical to run. Where individual gas boilers are used in flat developments care must be taken in locating the supply meter in the flat as the gas authority will insist on running the supply to upper floors externally, an aesthetic problem for designers to resolve. Alternatively, the supply meters may be located all together in an intake room, with individual supplies running from the meters to the flats – but this is an expensive and potentially dangerous solution.

The installation of gas in sheltered housing is subject to debate as it can be a hazard when used by the forgetful. In rented schemes with centralised boilers, it is common to use gas for heating, with only electricity supplied direct to the flats. However, in schemes for some ethnic minorities such as the Chinese or other Asians, gas is the only fuel which will satisfactorily provide the rapid temperature changes required by stir-frying cooking techniques.

Oil-fired systems are only suitable for centralised heating schemes; usually these are only used where gas is not available and electricity not considered suitable.

Electricity, using storage heaters run from cheaper off-peak demand supplies, is a flexible and easy to instal heat source. Storage heaters cannot be used in bathrooms as they are a source of danger. The only solution for this room is to use an 'on peak' heater at high level. Despite improvements in the design of electrical storage units they are still relatively bulky, taking up floor space.

Where centralised systems are used, it is advisable to locate the plant room at the centre of the scheme to minimise the length of distribution pipework. For most developments distribution pipework is best run through the ground floor corridor at high level. The pipework will require a duct depth of approximately 350 mm (14 in). The false ceiling covering the pipework must be demountable for future servicing, and access to control valves must be identified.

Heating systems must be designed to provide the following temperatures, based on an external temperature of $-1°C$ with a mean system temperature of $77°C$ and a natural air change rate of 1 per hour in all areas:

Dwellings, guest room, shower, laundry and common room	21°C
Warden's office	18°C
Entrance foyer, corridors and staircases	16°C

Where central hot water storage is provided, it should be designed on the basis of 22 litres per person with a recovery period of 2 hours.

2. Water supply

The local water authority must be consulted on the volume of cold water to be stored and asked to define the requirements in respect of the incoming water supply to the site or dwellings. In many cases recently water authorities have insisted that in rented accommodation individual supplies be taken to each flat, because of the possibility of tenants having the 'right to purchase' in the future. In centralised schemes the distribution pipes can be conveniently run in the roof space with drops to lower floors through kitchens and bathrooms. Local systems, and flats for sale, must be served via individual external stop cocks. Combination cold and hot water storage cylinders provide suitable water storage for individual systems. Care must be taken to select taps suitable for use by possibly arthritic fingers: avoid heads that do not offer an easy grip, using instead lever heads or cross-headed hand wheels. Ceramic disc washers are available in some taps which require only a half-turn to operate the valve and have a longer life than normal tap washers. These taps are more expensive but they save on maintenance and are far easier to use.

3. Lighting

Here design must be functional, providing a level of illumination appropriate for the situation and the activities being carried out. At the same time it should be creative, highlighting features and adding interest to rooms and circulation areas. Much can be done in the entrance foyer of flats to set the character of the whole scheme. Is it institutional or welcoming?

Corridor lighting must be carefully designed to avoid a regiment of fittings, lights, emergency lights and smoke detectors marching away into the distance. General lighting in corridors can be obtained successfully by the use of wall lights beside the entrance doors and delivery shelves to flats.

The level of illumination to communal areas, measured at a height of 1 m above floor level, should be as follows:

Common rooms generally and entrance foyer	300 lux
Hobbies rooms and laundry	500 lux
Corridors, staircases, boiler room	150 lux
Other plant rooms	100 lux

Basically, all illumination levels should be in accordance with the recommendations of the Code of the I.E.S. (Illuminating Engineers Society).

Lighting in corridors and staircases must be circuited for the following conditions:

Daytime	Reinforce illumination where natural light is inadequate
Dusk to midnight	Full lighting throughout
Midnight to dawn	Minimum safety lighting

Emergency lighting should be provided to all escape routes in accordance with the recommendations of CP 5266. Emergency luminaires should be connected to come into operation upon mains or sub-circuit failure. For schemes requiring up to 25 luminaires, the self-contained type are most economical as far as installation costs are concerned. Above this number it is worth considering a central battery unit system, but this requires a separate room or location with adequate natural ventilation. Individual self-contained luminaires have an average life span of approximately five years for their integral batteries, whereas a central battery system, properly maintained, will have a life span of up to 25 years. Emergency luminaires cannot be used for night lighting unless they are of the maintained type, having a mains and battery supply source. All emergency fittings should have a test facility to ensure that they are operational.

Light and power for individual dwellings should be provided via a metered supply situated in a metal consumer cabinet outside the entrance door to the dwelling.

The supply authority must be consulted on the height at which these consumer cabinets should be mounted, as requirements vary.

Within the dwelling the following *minimum* lighting and power points should be provided:

Lobby	1 lighting point
Living room	1 lighting point, 4 power points
Bedroom	1 lighting point, 2 power points
Bathroom	1 lighting point
Kitchen	1 lighting point, 4 power points and 1 cooker point

The lighting to the kitchen is best provided by a fluorescent lamp, and shadows under wall fittings should be avoided. Designers should examine different furnishing layouts for each room to ensure that switches and power points are not likely to be obstructed by furniture or door swings. As a general rule power points, which must be individually switched, should not be situated less than 450 mm (18 in) from internal corners and they must be located 1000 mm (40 in) above the floor level. Light switches must be the flush-mounted rocker type; do not use ceiling pull cords as they may be confused with alarm cords. Stores and internal bathrooms should have external switches incorporating a neon indicator to avoid lights being left on unnecessarily.

4. Lifts

For the active elderly, access to first floor flats via a gentle staircase does not present any difficulty; however, today's active elderly may well be tomorrow's frail elderly, for whom stairs will become a problem. As we are designing to avoid the distress for our clients of being forced to move into different accommodation later on, it is prudent to provide a lift in all flat developments. As advised earlier, the lift should be situated near to the entrance foyer, and the shaft must be isolated from habitable rooms to prevent structurally borne noise causing annoyance.

The hydraulic general purpose lift of 600 kg (1323 pounds) per 8-person capacity, providing an entrance opening of not less than 800 mm (32 in) wide by 2000 mm (80 in) high, has been found to be best in practice. The smallest lift-car size must permit accommodation for a wheelchair and attendant. Most hydraulic lifts require a hydraulic ram to be sunk below the lift pit, the depth being determined by the number of storeys being served. Rams mounted on the lift pit floor can be provided but they are more expensive. A pump room associated with the lift shaft must be provided. This is normally at ground floor level adjacent to the shaft, and may usefully be situated some distance away: the lift manufacturers will advise on the maximum distance but generally 5 m (16.5 ft) is possible.

Landing and lift-car doors should be of the automatic sliding type, with an automatic facility to hold the door open while anyone is entering or exiting. Cellulosing the lift doors a bright colour will help some residents locate the lift and avoid recourse to a plethora of signs.

The lift-car interior should be equipped with a handrail at the rear 915 mm (36 in) above floor level, a self-contained emergency light, natural ventilation, and a control panel with floor selectors, alarm and door hold pushes set 1200 mm (48 in) above the floor. In addition to the general alarm required in accordance with the Code of Practice, it is suggested that the warning device be sited at ground floor level adjacent to the lift entrance door. As well as this alarm, it is recommended that a connection, via a trailing cable, be incorporated in the warden call system to enable a speech unit to be fitted in each lift car, so that in an emergency situation the warden can communicate with persons in the car.

As a general rule all houses designed for the elderly should provide accommodation that can be adapted simply to enable the clients to 'stay put' when they can no longer use the stair. Bathroom and bedroom space should be available at ground floor level. Where this is not possible the stairway should be designed to permit the installation of a stairlift. For this to be a practical option, the ground and first floor landings must be large enough to accommodate the travelling seat.

5. Ventilation

All internal bathrooms, toilets, shower rooms, etc., must be provided with mechanical extract ventilation. Common room kitchens and laundries will also require mechanical ventilation. Where refuse collection or storage points are likely to be the source of smells, these spaces should also be mechanically ventilated, with the discharge at high level away from flats.

The internal bathrooms, toilets and showers should have six air changes per hour. Two-speed extract fans operated by the light switch, having one speed continuous and a second speed with a twenty-minute overrun, are the most suitable. A 10 mm (0.4 in) gap must be left under the entrance door to ensure a proper air change and avoid unequal air pressure burning out the fan motor. The position of the discharge air should be designed to avoid nuisance.

Communications

Emergency alarms

As they age, the clients are more at risk of falling and needing help but not being able to contact anyone. Statistical evidence shows that although the young elderly are only marginally more at risk than the 45–64 age group, those over 75 are more likely to have a fatal accident at home. Sixty-eight per cent of all fatal domestic accidents involve those over 65, with the 75 + group being most at risk.[2] For the isolated and lonely this may mean lying for days unable to obtain help. The presence of a telephone does not help where the nature of the injury caused by the fall makes it impossible to reach the instrument, which may be positioned at a high level, possibly in another room. A wide range of trigger mechanisms and alarm functions have been developed to help combat this problem. There are three broad groups of alarm to be considered, each group having optional facilities.

(a) Warden call alarms

The warden call alarm system is common in most sheltered housing schemes, with the facility for two-way speech being most favoured. This enables the warden to call the residents once a day to see if all is well. The system centres on a master unit under the control of the warden. Portable master units with jack sockets in the warden's home, office and guest room provide flexibility in use. When the warden is on holiday, a temporary warden may use the guest room with the master unit to hand. For further flexibility jack sockets can be incorporated in the residents' sub-units, enabling the warden to make contact whilst visiting residents. Within the residents' dwellings the sub-unit should be located in the living room or lobby. The sub-unit should be capable of receiving speech and transmitting through two closed doors to ensure that audible contact can be made in the event of an accident where the resident is unable to go to the sub-unit. Facilities for triggering the alarm should be located in the living room, bedroom and bathroom. The living-room trigger should be close to the kitchen door. An alarm once triggered should set off visual indicators outside the flat door and in the warden's office, where they should also be visible from the entrance foyer. It is common practice to provide a sub-unit in the entrance foyer and communal rooms, with trigger facilities in common WCs and the shower room.

(b) Group or communal alarms

Where there is no resident warden to receive an alarm call, as in Category 1 schemes, a communal alarm system may be used. This functions by a trigger mechanism setting off an audible alarm and visual indicator alerting neighbours to the emergency. The system can be improved by relaying the signal via an unmanned unit on the site to a control centre. With a two-way speech system incorporated, the personal contact provides peace of mind with the knowledge that the alarm has been received and action is being taken.

(c) Dispersed alarms

Dispersed alarm systems give protection for isolated clients who do not enjoy the support of a warden or a group scheme. In this case the alarm trigger is linked to a control centre manned 24 hours a day. Such systems may also provide evening and night-time coverage in Category 2 schemes, enabling the warden to function within more clearly defined working hours.

(d) Trigger systems

Trigger systems vary from ceiling-mounted pull cords or wall-mounted push buttons to personal portable triggers. For fixed situations the pull cord with a ring suspended 150 mm (6 in) above the floor gives an injured person a reasonable chance of reaching and sounding the alarm. Personal triggers, worn either around the neck or wrist, have the advantage that a fall away from a fixed alarm point can be easily triggered, and this is a significant benefit for the 75 + group. However, not everyone will have the patience to wear one and the triggers can be mislaid. The relationship of ceiling-mounted alarm pull cords to possible furniture layouts must be carefully considered, especially in the living room and bedrooms where most accidents occur.[3] Pull cords in the wrong position are positively dangerous. Appendix B (p. 000) gives some key dimensions.

The alarm system may also include optional functions such as smoke detectors, room temperature detectors, intruder alarms and pressure mats.

[2]British National Statistics, *Home Accident Surveillance System*, compiled by the Department of Trade and Industry

[3]*Dispersed Alarms: A guide for organisations installing systems*, Research Institute for Consumer Affairs, 1986

MEANS OF ESCAPE, FIRE PRECAUTIONS, SERVICES AND COMMUNICATIONS

Consideration must be given to what the response will be in the event of an emergency, and also to how access will be obtained if the client is immobile. One solution is to provide an electronic door release operated by the alarm trigger. Regrettably, with the incidence of crime rising, many old people install additional security door locks which frustrate the door release system.

Telephones

All schemes should be provided with conduit and draw wires for telephone installation. The instrument is best located in the living room of each dwelling.

Television aerials

A central aerial must be provided and the signal amplified for distribution to TV socket outlets in each dwelling. The possible furniture layouts must be considered to determine the best location for each socket outlet and, as described previously, to permit comfortable daytime viewing.

7 RETIREMENT OR SHELTERED HOUSING?

Integral to the concept of sheltered housing is the idea, not only that the elderly need a home that they can manage, which is easy to maintain and user-friendly, but that a degree of care is required to support their independence. It has been argued that if the element of care involves the presence of a warden or housekeeper, then independence has already been surrendered. However, this notion cannot be substantiated and must be considered as a subjective response to the presence of any authority. Help and assistance is necessary at all levels of ageing and no one need feel dependent if his or her flat is under the management of a company, with a caretaker or porter to look after day-to-day maintenance problems.

Degrees of care to support independence

The role of a warden or housekeeper can be specified to meet specific levels of care, either as a background presence responsible for the general management of the building, or as a higher profile activity which involves ensuring that the day-to-day needs of the residents are catered for, with support agencies (nursing, domestic, etc.) employed to meet those needs. The threshold between housing for the elderly with community care, and 'sheltered housing', is crossed once residential care, to whatever degree, is introduced. As discussed in Chapter 2, the degree of residential care can be minimal or service-rich and the degree of care proposed will affect the design of the building.

The range of housing designed specifically for the aged, and this encompasses anyone over the age of 55, has in the past decade expanded to include retirement housing without any residential care at one end of the spectrum, to very sheltered housing for the frail elderly at the other. Commercial developments of sheltered housing in the UK have generated in excess of 31,000 units in some 900 schemes, and growth is forecast at a rate in excess of 20,000 units per annum.[1] The development of dispersed alarm systems has made possible small sheltered housing schemes without a resident warden. These dispersed alarm systems have also demonstrated that, given a suitable home and environment with support and shopping facilities nearby, the elderly can stay put if they so wish. 'Sheltered' in this context means being able to call for assistance in an emergency. Commercial developers and house builders have tapped into a growth market, where the scale of development and the attractions of this type of housing for all socio-economic groups are perceived to be almost unlimited, with luxury flats and houses planned in the salubrious suburbs of London, and villages of more than 400 units proposed in the countryside.

---

[1] Baker, S. and Parry, M., *Housing for sale to the elderly: a review of the retirement housing market and future trends*, Housing Research Foundation, 1986

Continuing care

The range of care on offer has expanded to include nursing homes as part of sheltered housing schemes: the 'continuing care' market generally has attracted a lot of commercial attention. Housing associations with existing populations of ageing residents are at the front end of coping with the problem of caring for the frail elderly, and the main trend of future housing association developments is likely to be in the direction of providing for this group.

Integrated care

In questioning conventional sheltered housing wisdom, Fisk[2] puts forward the idea of an 'integrated sheltered housing model', according to which the design of the building would make it largely indistinguishable from other housing types, and its resources would be expanded to cater for higher levels of disabilities for all age groups, rendering the scheme a community resource. He argues that, by using wardens more effectively, the frail elderly could stay put within the scheme and local elderly could be served in their own homes. The integrated model is an interesting idea but in its emphasis on the scheme as a resource centre it has shifted a long way from the original housing concept and entered the field of community care. A centre of this type would not be segregated from the community by age but by ability, or more significantly by physical disability.

Responding to a variety of needs

We have referred to 'staying put', an option open to those fortunate enough to live in the right locality and in a suitable house, and have considered Categories 1 and 2 housing and the fast developing trend of housing the frail elderly in Category $2\frac{1}{2}$ schemes. The variety of sheltered housing options has arisen from the range of decisions possible on what degree of care should be provided and whether the care should be residential or peripatetic.

The idea of 'continuing care' and the 'integrated' models of sheltered housing are seen as blurring the 'category' edges of housing for the elderly and providing a whole life support system. Whether these ideas would meet with social acceptance is open to question. Most elderly people entering sheltered housing stay there until they die, and studies by Heuman[3] show that there is little movement along the continuum from housing the active elderly to full residential care. The conveyor-belt notion of housing for diminishing mobility and ability overlooks the basic wish of the elderly to have a permanent home of their own with help on hand if they require it. What is required is a variety of different accommodation suitable for different degrees of disability, with services either on site or off site which may be called on when required. The movement of elderly people from their family homes into sheltered housing will occur at different levels of age and disability and our housing stock should cater for this. To quote Boldy[4], 'Don't put all your eggs in one basket'. There is a place in the market for all the options on sheltered housing that we have discussed.

---

[2] Fisk, J. M., *Independence and the elderly*, Croom Helm, 1986

[3] Heumann, L. F., 'The function of different sheltered housing categories for the semi-independent elderly', *Social Policy and Administration*, Vol. 15, No. 2, Summer 1981

[4] Boldy, D., 'Don't put all your eggs in one basket', *Community Care*, No. 447, 27 January 1983

8 | CASE STUDIES

The buildings examined in this chapter reflect the wide range of accommodation, in size, privacy and service, provided by sheltered housing.

The scheme at Wye is typical of a small-scale development of retirement dwellings built to Category 1 standards. In most respects the buildings are similar to ordinary housing, but they differ in two important respects. Firstly, all the dwellings are built to full mobility standards and for ease of use by the infirm. Where stairs are introduced they are either shared in common stairways for safety reasons, or, as in the case of the cottages, the upper floor is only designed as guest accommodation. Secondly, provision of alarm cords gives peace of mind, in the knowledge that aid can be called.

Harwell is a typical small Category 2 scheme with a resident warden. It is interesting to compare this building with the scheme at Daventry where extra-care facilities have been provided, increasing the possibility of residents remaining in their own homes. At Harwell the elderly are expected to cook and care for themselves. For those residents who find bathing difficult there is a shower room. At Daventry the care is extended to include the provision of assisted bathing, and hot meals are provided for those experiencing difficulty in cooking.

A scheme for the Abbeyfield Housing Association is included in the case studies as a contrast to the normal categories of sheltered housing. Here the housing philosophy is quite different. In the Abbeyfield Houses, the elderly live as small family groups, sharing a kitchen and bathroom with a resident housekeeper.

The most ambitious scheme included is at Almere in the Netherlands. With the exception of resident nursing care every facility is available. All the dwellings are self-contained, with accommodation for both active and frail elderly. Support services include resident staff, and meals which are served either in the restaurant or delivered to the flats.

Category 1: Sheltered housing at Wye, Kent

Architects: Francis Weal & Partners

Client: Guardian Housing Association

The site is a narrow strip of land with an access drive shared with the village library and the university student hostel. It is close to local shopping and a wide range of facilities. Because of the limitation of the site, single-aspect cottages were designed, overlooking the pedestrian access which leads to two-storey flats at the end of the site. As there is no resident warden, the group is self-supporting in the sense that the public outdoor space, the pedestrian access, is overlooked by most of the dwellings to provide a measure of 'defensible' space and also to enable the residents to keep a friendly eye on their neighbours coming and going.

There are four cottages, each with a floor area of 68.80 m² (740 sq ft). The cottages provide a living room, kitchen, bedroom and bathroom at ground floor level and a second bedroom in the roof

Fig. 46 Pedestrian access with four-person houses in the foreground. (Photo: Photo-Flair Ltd)

Fig. 47 Entrance to two-person flats. (Photo: Photo-Flair Ltd)

CASE STUDIES

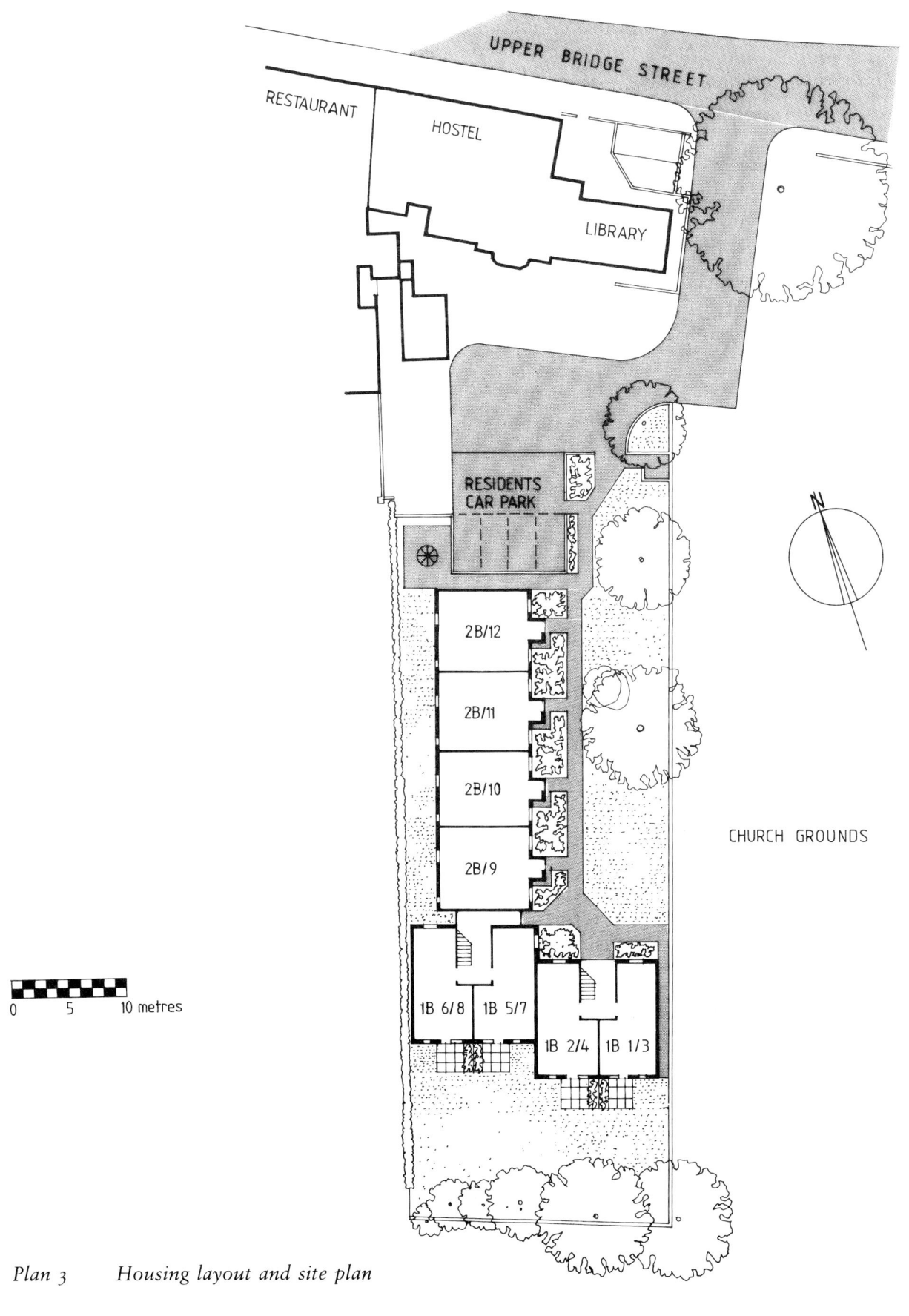

Plan 3   Housing layout and site plan

CASE STUDIES

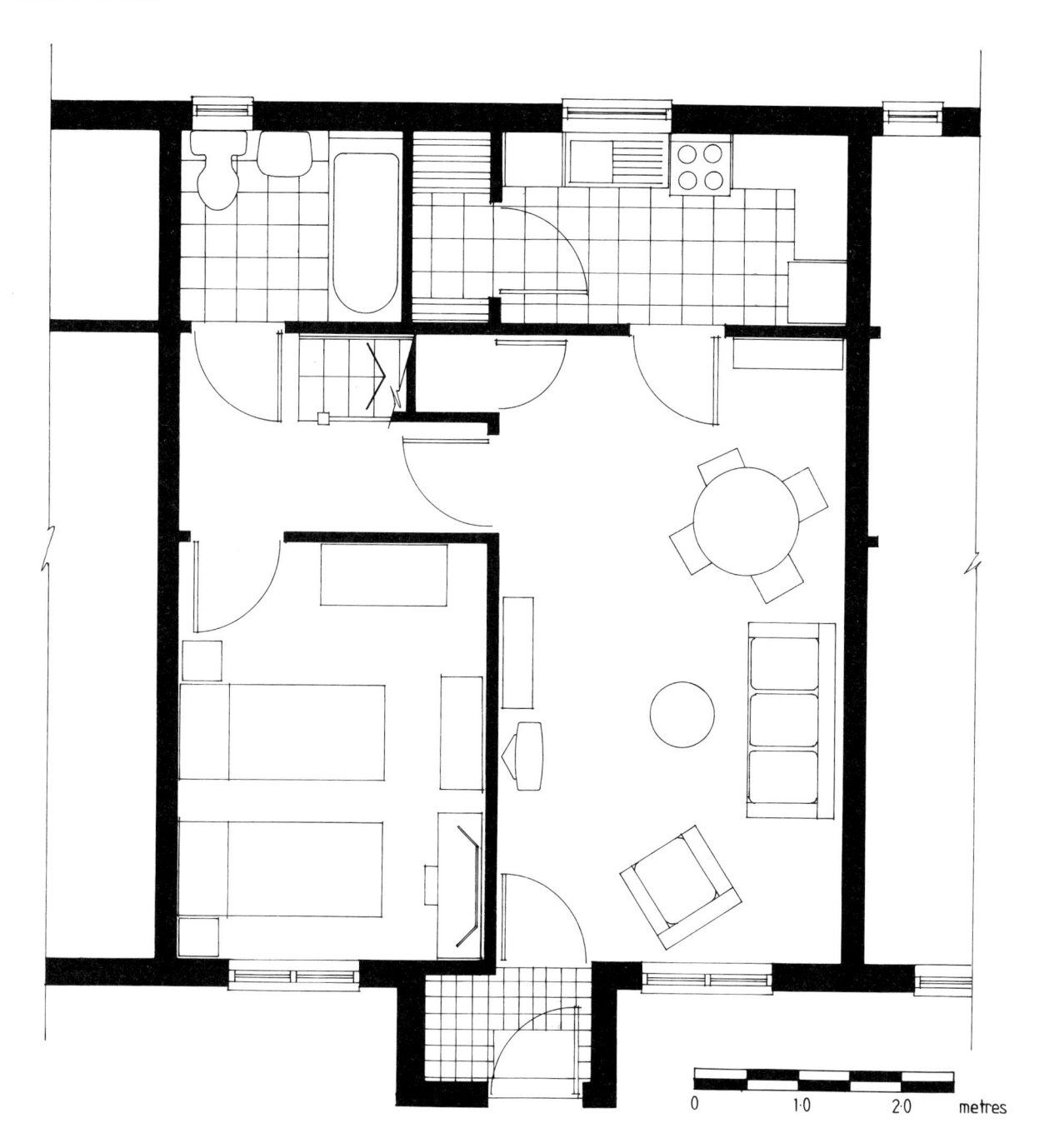

Plan 4   Four-person house ground floor plan

space. The roof space also provides additional storage. With this layout the frail elderly or handicapped can enjoy the benefit of living at ground floor level, without recourse to the stair, and have a guest bedroom at first floor level.

The eight flats are grouped around two public stairwells, each stairway having an easy rise and going. With four flats sharing a stairwell it is unlikely that any resident suffering a fall on the stair would be left for any length of time without aid being called. The flats are designed for two persons each, with the bedroom large enough to accommodate separate beds. The floor area of each flat is 42.16 m² (453 sq ft). The cottages and

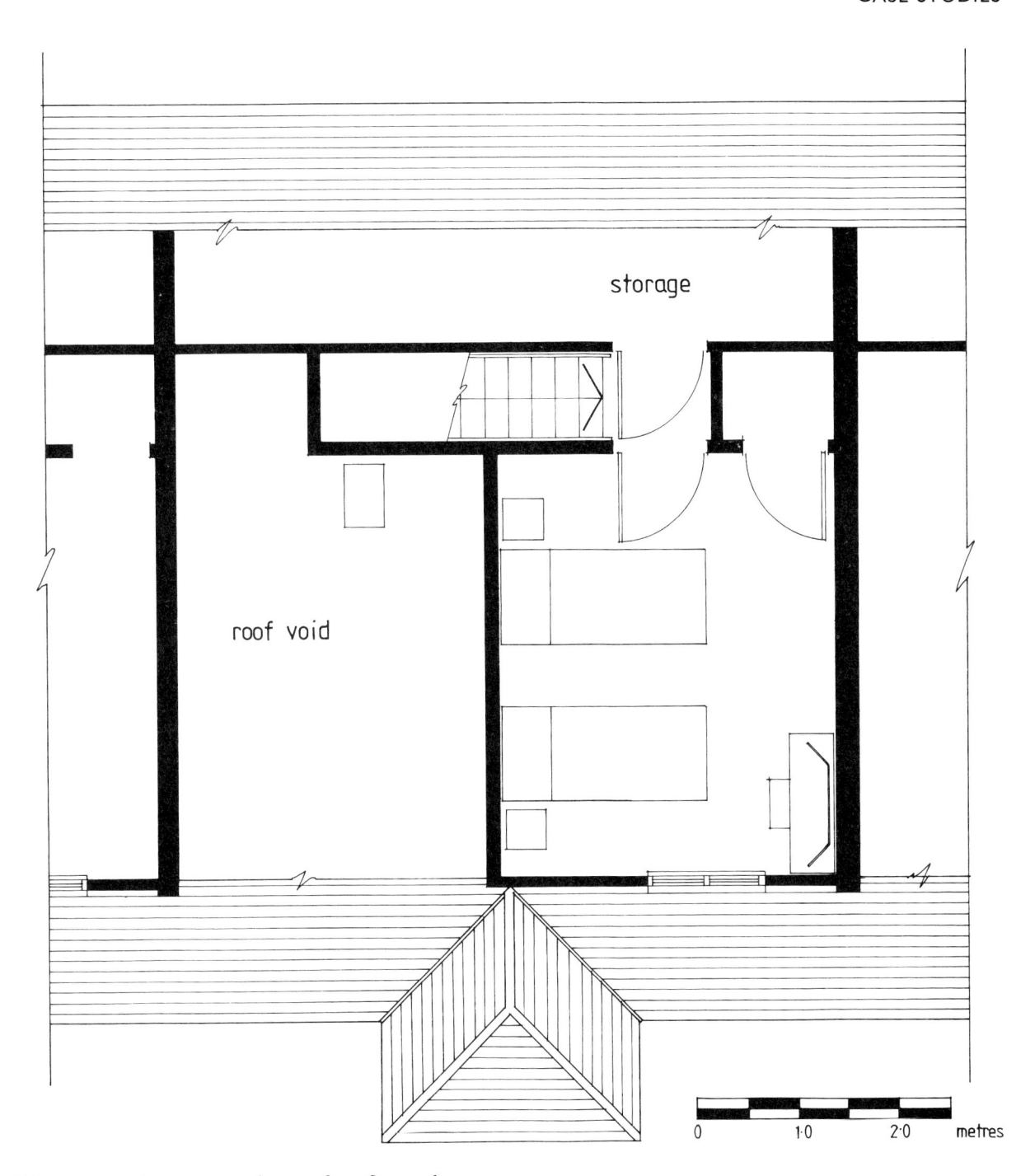

Plan 5   Four-person house first floor plan

flats are designed to full mobility standards with alarm cords fitted in the bathrooms, bedrooms and living rooms. These alarms activate an external flashing beacon to the cottages and a flashing beacon in the stairwell of the flats to attract attention and alert passers-by to an emergency.

Group administration is provided by the housing association and a warden visits the residents from time to time.

CASE STUDIES

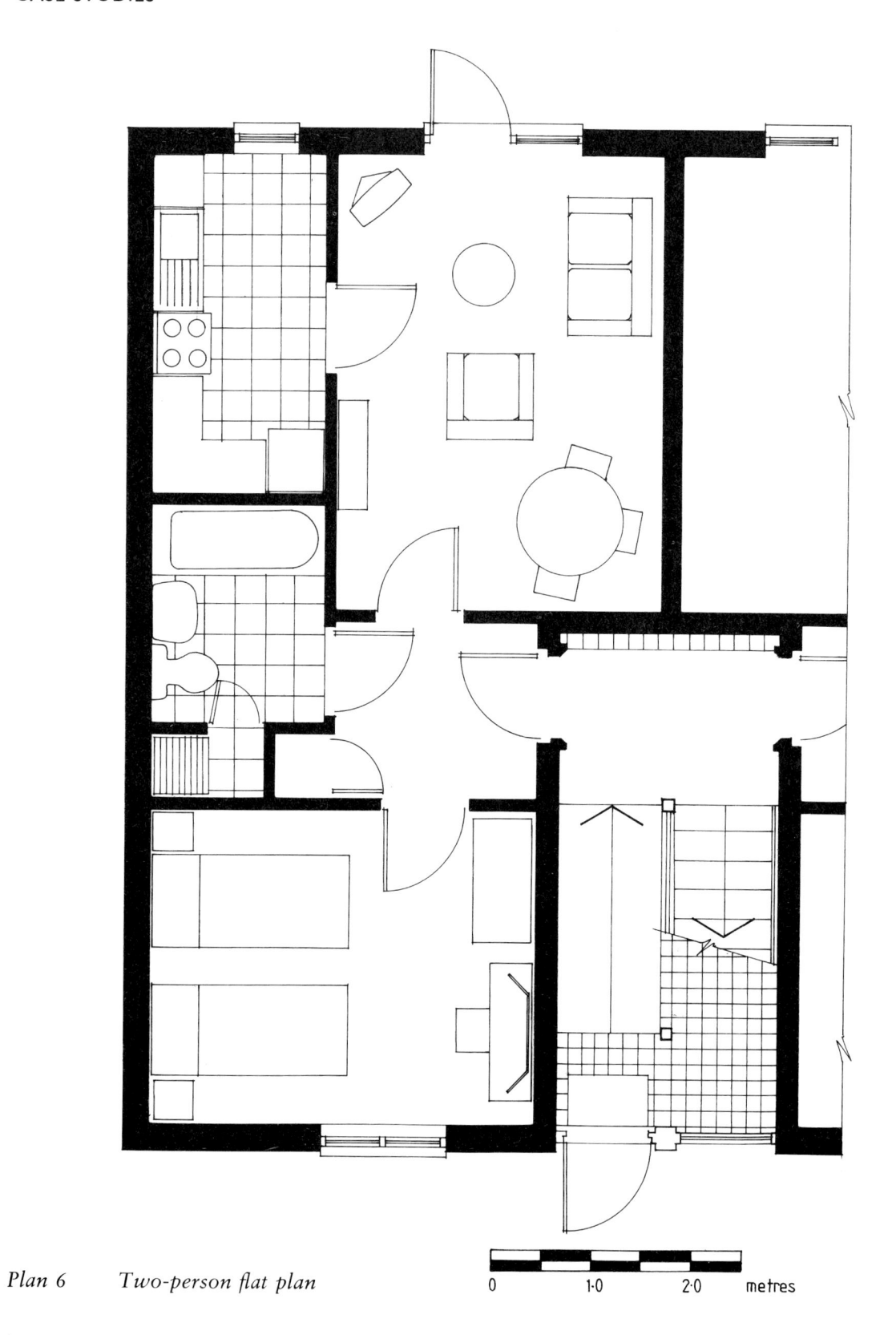

Plan 6   Two-person flat plan

Category 2: Sheltered housing at Harwell, Oxfordshire

Architects: Francis Weal & Partners

Client: Anchor Housing Association

The site, which was formerly part of the vicarage garden, has an area of 0.28 ha (0.69 acres). The development was funded by the local authority who were anxious to provide a scheme, with a resident warden, to full Category 2 standards and with as many two-person flats as possible. This posed special problems as the site area and planning constraints limited the size of the building to 21 flats (10 one-person and 11 two-person flats) and a warden's flat.

The ratio of flats to warden fell way below the optimum ratio of 30:1, so the design solution had to be economic to keep the residents' overheads of a warden, common room, guest room, etc. to an acceptable level.

A cruciform-plan shape was adopted, with the one lift and stair located centrally, serving the four wings. The lift shaft was isolated structurally from the adjacent flat. As there is no alternative means of escape in case of fire at first floor level, a smoke dispersal installation was provided, with windows opening automatically in the corridors when triggered by the smoke detectors located throughout the corridors.

Apart from its small size, this scheme is a typical Category 2 project, complete with warden, common room, pantry, guest room, laundry, shower room and public telephone.

The one-person flats have a floor area of 34.18 m² (368 sq ft). The kitchens are planned with enough space for the preparation of food and for a small table and chairs suitable for informal meals. No units are positioned under the kitchen window, so that it can easily be opened and shut. The single bedroom is planned as a rectangular space with a minimum dimension of 2.6 m (8 ft 6 ins). This permits various ways of positioning the bed. For ease of bedmaking some residents prefer the island position so that they may get around to both sides, while others are happy to have the length of the bed against the wall.

The two-person flats have a floor area of 42.7 m² (460 sq ft). As in the one-person flats there is space for eating in the kitchen and easy access to the window.

The warden's flat is strategically planned over the common room to allow a discreet view of people coming and going. A separate warden's entrance is designed for the privacy of the warden's family. The rear boundary of the site is defined by a stream and mature trees. The garden by this boundary includes a pond which has been retained, and the landscape has been structured as a 'wild garden', a habitat encouraging flora and fauna for the interest of the residents. A local horticultural society has volunteered to help with the future maintenance of the wild garden, and this local interest in the scheme provides opportunities for integrating the resident elderly into the local community.

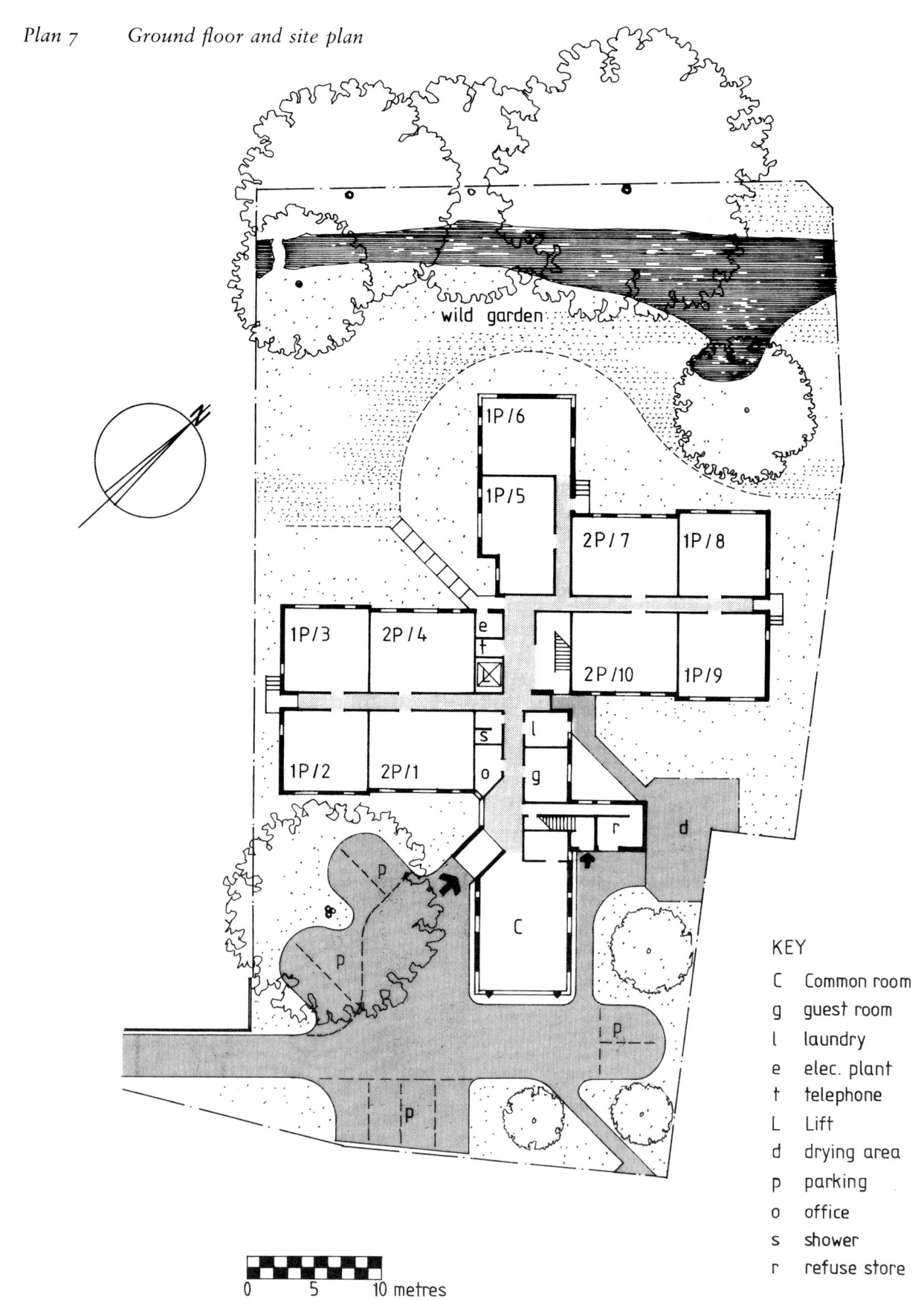

CASE STUDIES

Plan 7   Ground floor and site plan

108

CASE STUDIES

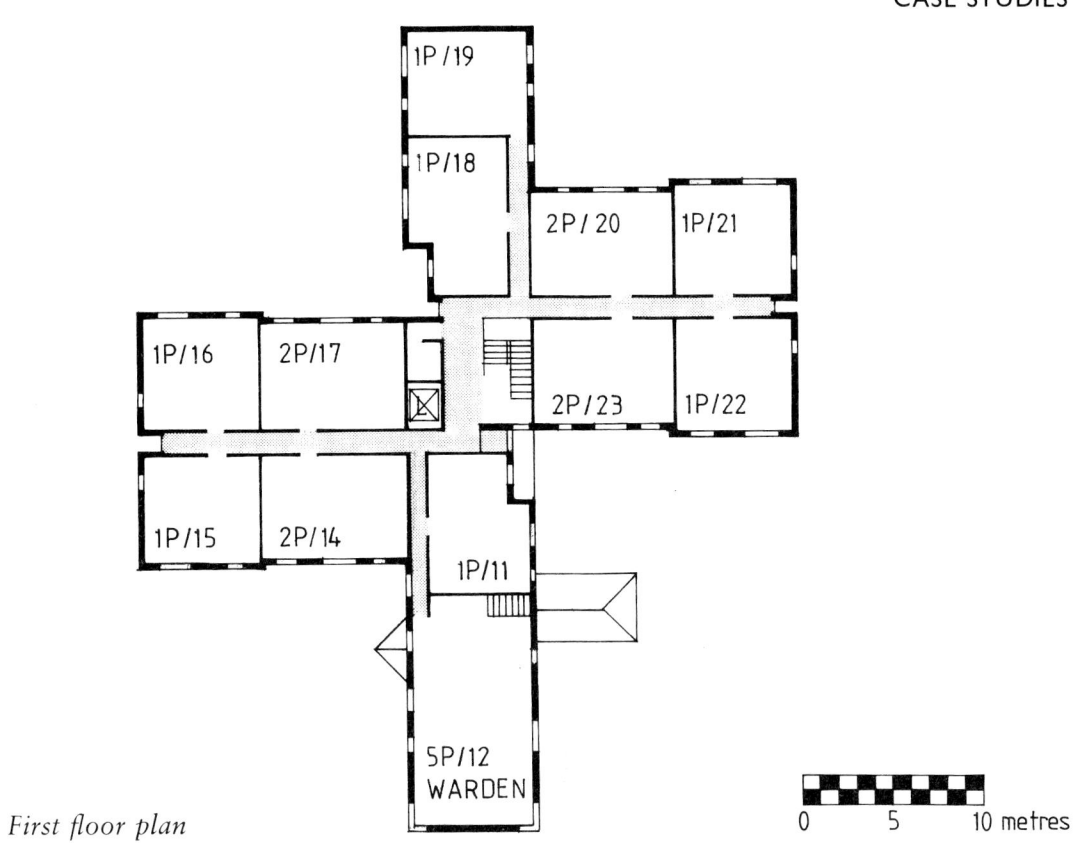

Plan 8   First floor plan

Fig. 48   *View of the combined vehicular and pedestrian entrance. (Photo: Alan Williams)*

CASE STUDIES

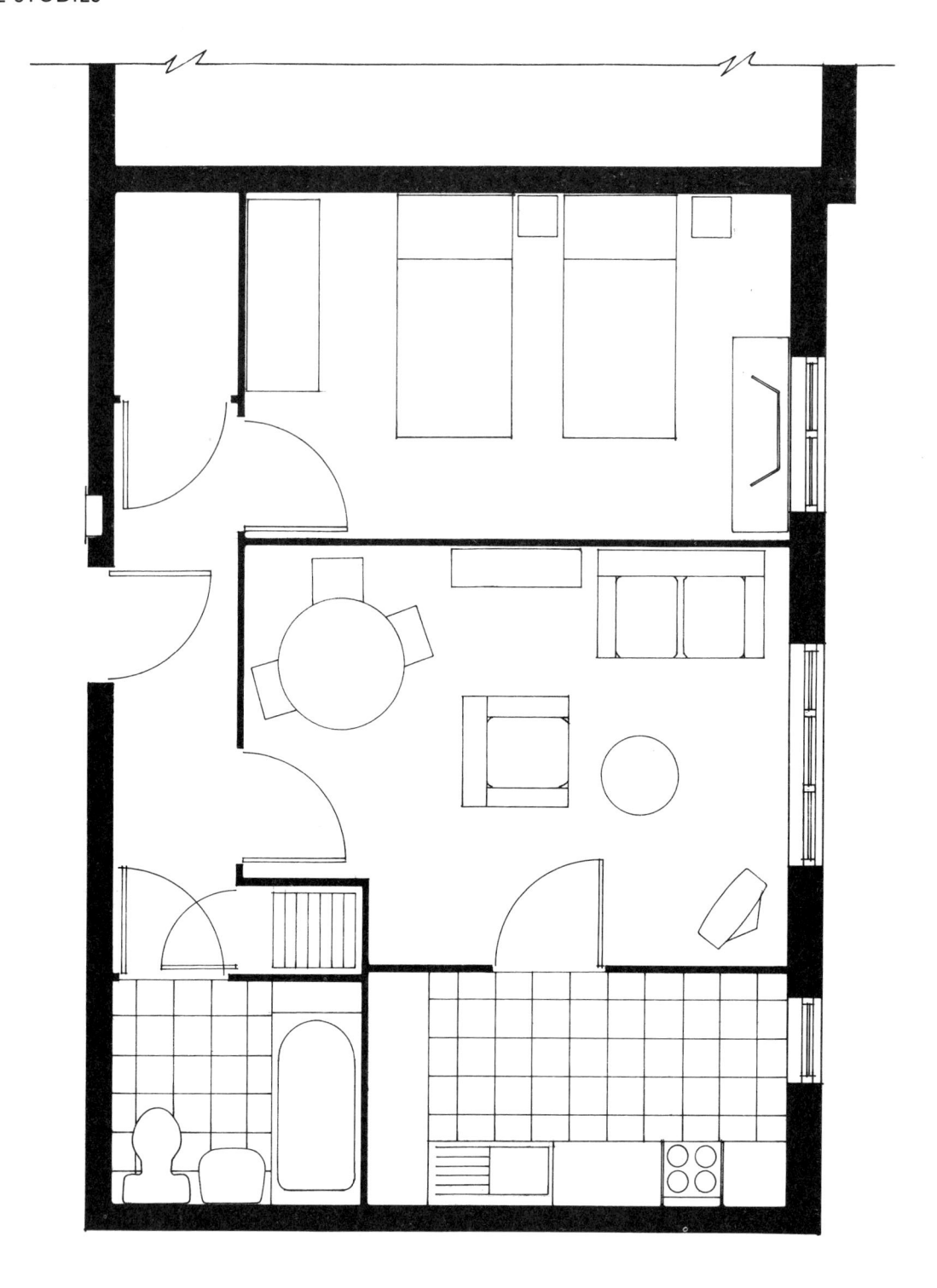

Plan 9   *Two-person flat plan*

CASE STUDIES

Plan 10   One-person flat plan

CASE STUDIES

Category 2: Sheltered housing at Faversham, Kent

Architects: Francis Weal & Partners

Client: Anchor Housing Association

The site has an area of 0.184 ha (0.44 acres) and is an ideal one for sheltered housing, close to the centre of the town and adjoining the public library, with the post office on the opposite side of the road. The neighbouring houses are three and two storeys high.

The building is composed of two blocks, three storeys high on the road frontage and two storeys high at the rear. An enclosed link is provided at ground floor level and an open deck links the first floors.

The total accommodation provided is thirty flats for the elderly and a warden or housekeeper's flat. Four of the flats are two person/one bedroom units, and the remaining 26 are one person bed-sit flats. These bed-sit flats have a floor area of 30.2 m² (325 sq ft). They are typical of the first generation of single person flats built in accordance with the D.O.E. circular 82/69.

Fig. 49 Street view with the common room and entrance in the foreground. (Photo: Robert Wilkinson)

Subsequent single person flats, in publicly funded schemes, have a slightly larger floor area and a separate bedroom. The change to separate bedrooms was welcomed at the time as an improvement of amenity; however, the bed-sit flats do have some advantages which are worth considering. They are, for the infirm or frail, easier to live in. There is one less door to negotiate, and for those periods when the resident is bedfast life is more tolerable as television can still be enjoyed without having to make arrangements for moving the set, space is available for visitors and access to the kitchen is simpler.

All the standard features of a Category 2 scheme are provided. The common room is by the entrance, with views on to the street, and the link to the rear block is enlarged to provide seating space with access to a private terrace facing south.

The local planning authority insisted at the planning stage that 15 car parking spaces should be provided (ratio 1:2). It was agreed to provide five hard standing spaces, with the remaining ten spaces grassed over but available for future use if required. Ten years after the completion of the scheme none of the residents own cars and the five spaces have proved to be more than sufficient for residents. The greatest demand for car parking space has been from visitors, but a nearby public car park has now resolved this problem.

CASE STUDIES

NEWTON ROAD

LIBRARY

car parking

HOUSING

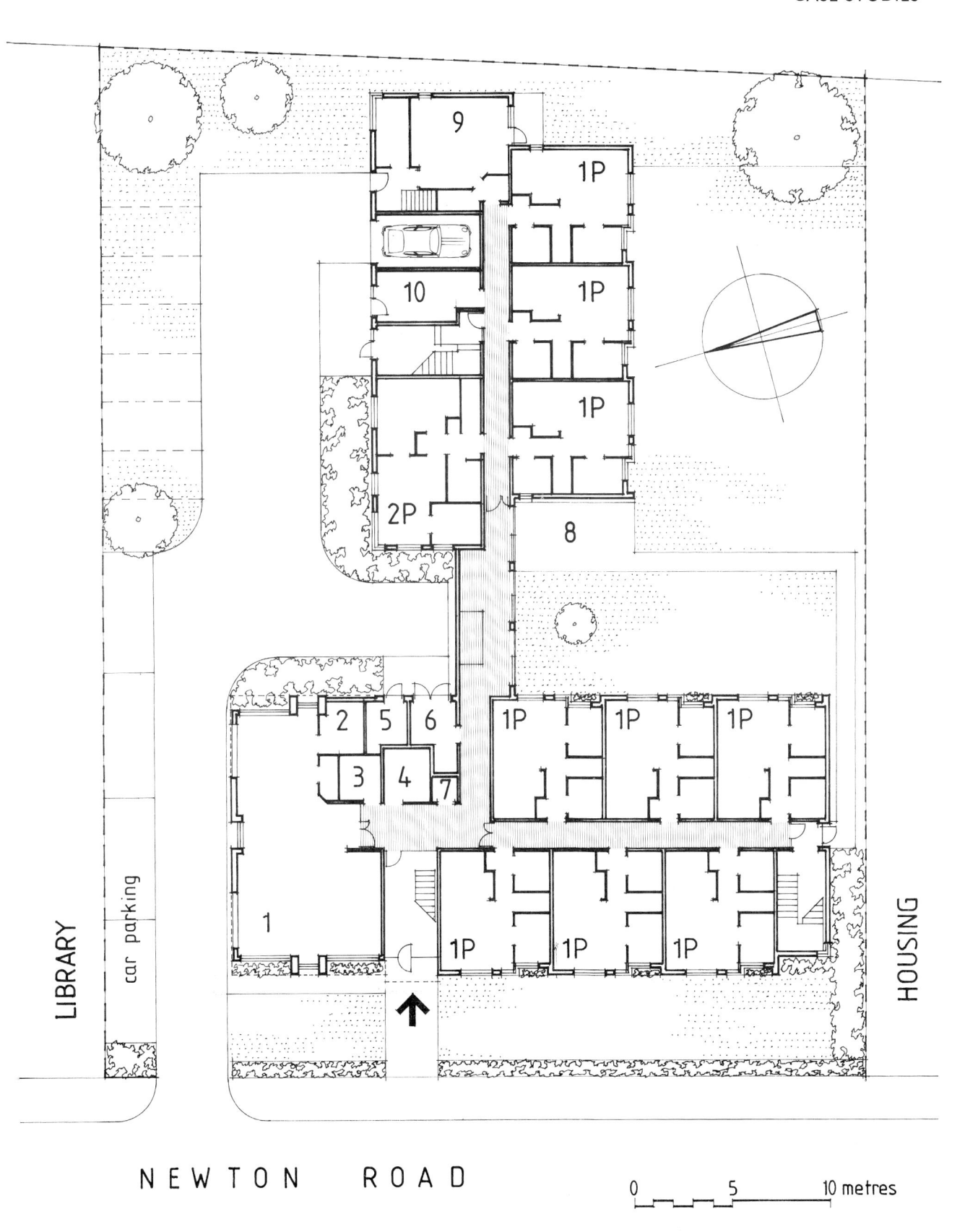

Plan 11   *Ground floor and site plan*

113

CASE STUDIES

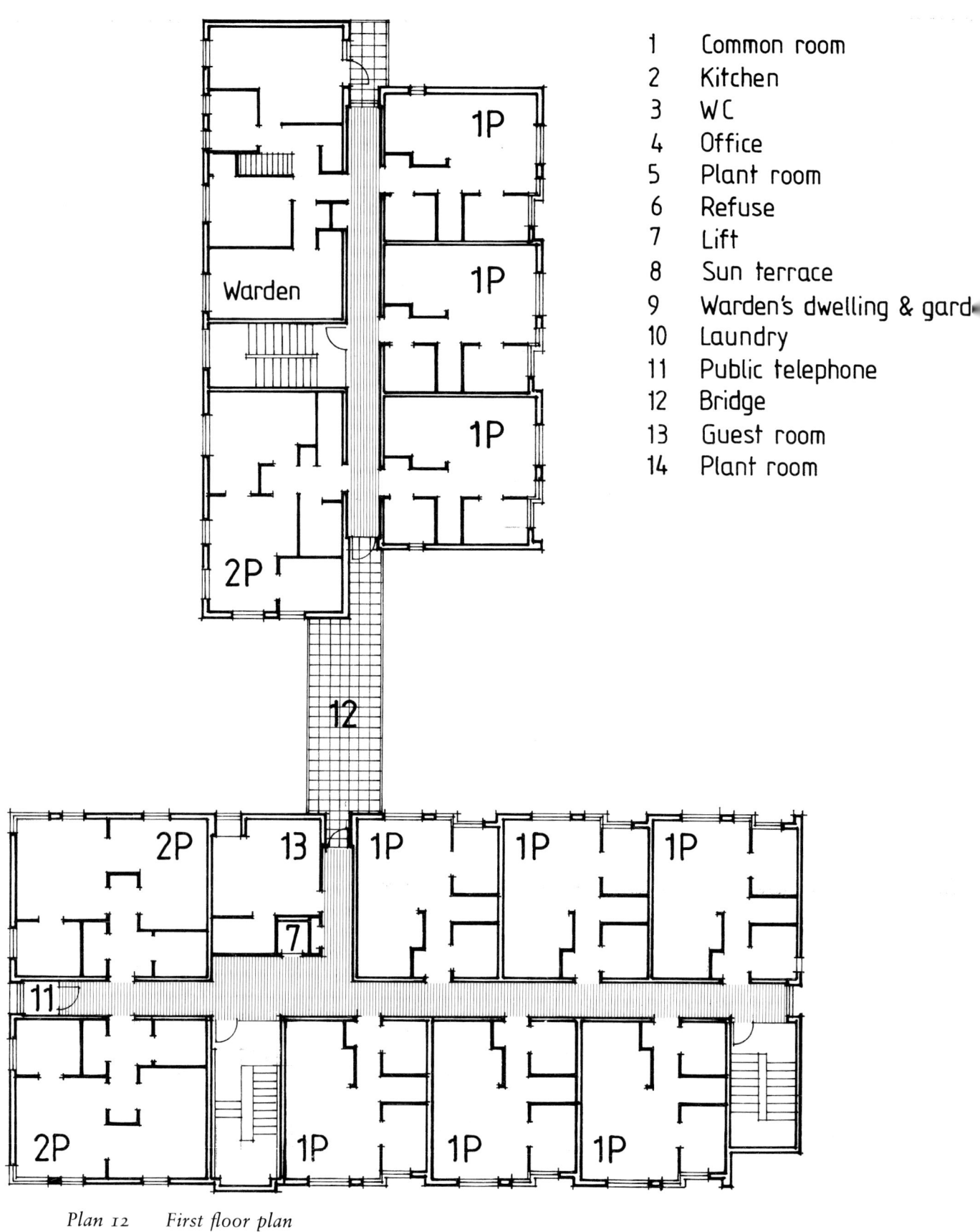

1	Common room
2	Kitchen
3	WC
4	Office
5	Plant room
6	Refuse
7	Lift
8	Sun terrace
9	Warden's dwelling & garden
10	Laundry
11	Public telephone
12	Bridge
13	Guest room
14	Plant room

Plan 12   First floor plan

CASE STUDIES

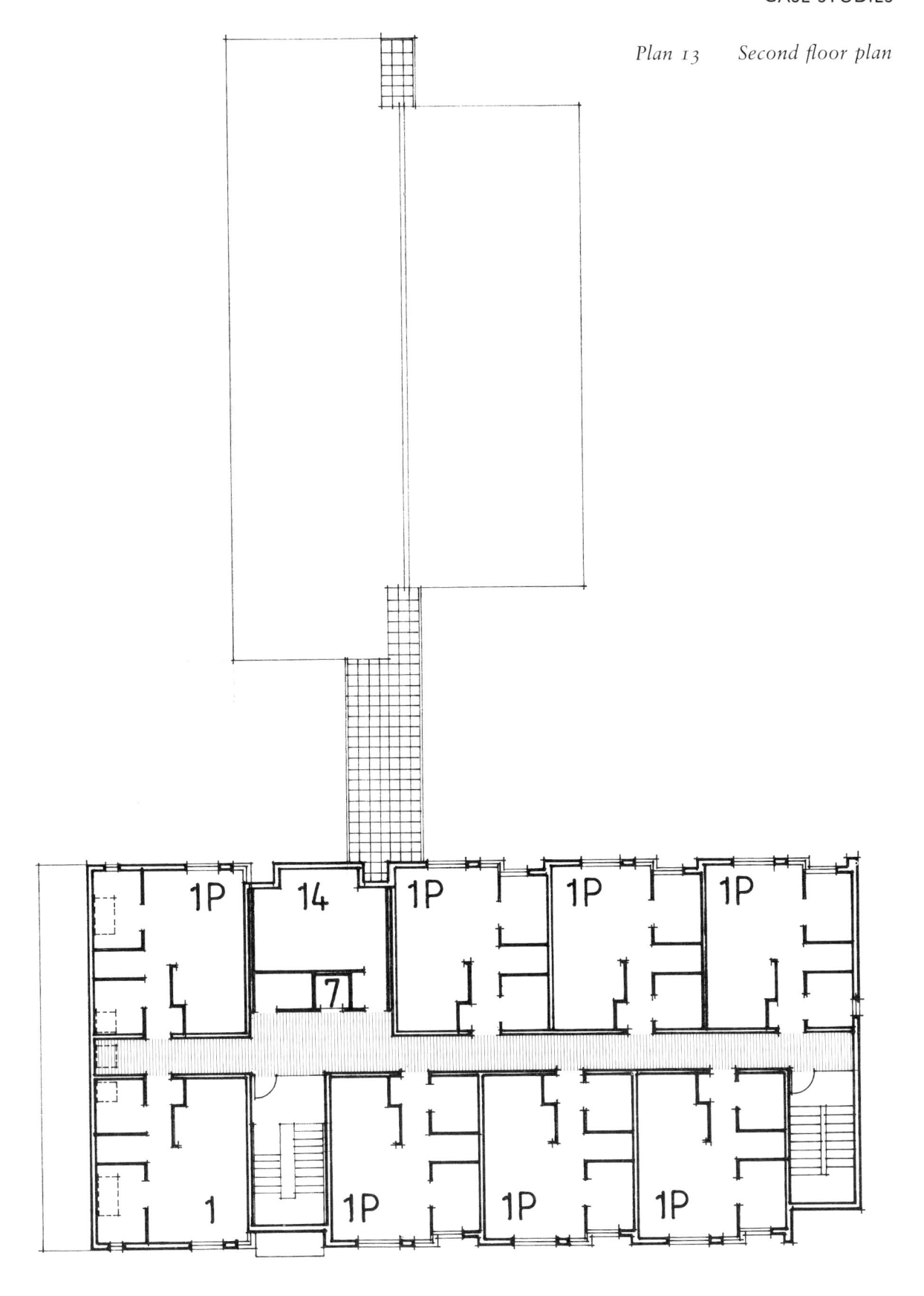

Plan 13   Second floor plan

CASE STUDIES

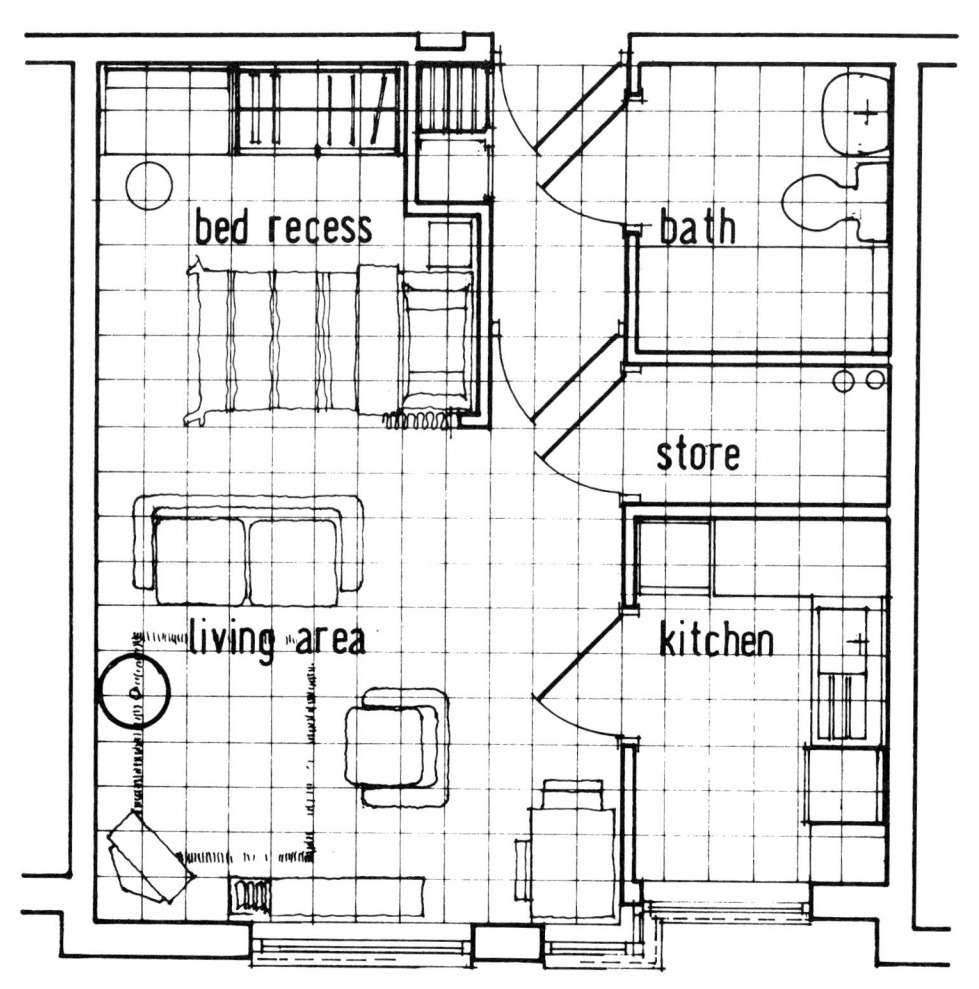

Plan 14   One-person bedsit flat

Fig. 50   Residents' private garden with access from the area linking the three and two storey wings. (Photo: Robert Wilkinson)

Category 2 (Extra-Care): Sheltered housing at Daventry, Northamptonshire

Architects: Phippen Randall and Parkes

Client: United Kingdom Housing Trust

This Category 2 scheme, containing extra-care facilities, is situated in Oxford Street, Daventry. It provides a total of 36 flats comprising 19 one-person flats and 17 two-person flats; in addition there are seven bungalows for the more active elderly. With 43 residential units to care for, provision has been made for two resident wardens to share the workload. The wardens enjoy their own private access and gardens. The ratio of car parking to dwellings approaches 1:2 and reflects the increased demand for parking spaces required in many locations.

With the exception of the warden's location, which does not provide views of the entrance area, the plan form is a model of the desirable distribution of spaces in a sheltered housing scheme.

The entrance is overlooked by the warden's office and enjoys a small seating area close by for residents awaiting transport or visitors. The lift, lavatories and common space are close to hand and the route from the lift to the laundry and refuse chamber is away from the entrance. By careful planning those parts of the building generating noise – the lift, refuse chamber, laundry, kitchen and boiler room – are structurally isolated from the flats.

In common with other schemes designed by this practice, the access routes are designed imaginatively, with recessed doorways and shelves inviting the residents to contribute to the decoration and furnishing of the space.

The extra-care facility includes a kitchen suitable for the preparation of hot meals, adjacent to a residents' dining area. This provision is not normal in most Category 2 schemes. In addition a special bathroom is provided at first floor level, close to the lift, for the convenience of residents requiring assistance whilst bathing. A small seating area adjacent to the special bathroom allows residents to meet informally whilst waiting for the lift or having an assisted bath. Additional facilities include a hairdressing room and guest room accommodation with a shower and lavatory en suite.

The common seating area is designed in two parts: a small quiet lounge, and a double height space facing south with an open fire built into the internal angle of the 'L' shape. This room avoids the institutional nature of many common rooms and takes on the character of a hotel lounge or foyer with the dining space opening off to one side. The plan form encourages informal grouping of seats and militates against regimentation of furniture.

A standard flat plan is used for the one-person flats, each having a floor area of 34.04 m² (366 sq ft). A feature of these flats is the use of mechanically ventilated internal kitchens with a window on to the corridor. This arrangement enables the living/dining room frontage to be increased to the benefit of the room's proportion. No provision is made for eating in the kitchen, nor is it shut off from the living room. This has the advantage that there is not a kitchen door to be negotiated, although this solution is not acceptable to everyone.

The two-person flats take two plan forms, A and B. Type A has a floor area of 41.37 m² (445 sq ft) and type B a floor area of 40 m² (430 sq ft). In common with the one-person flats the kitchen is en suite with the living/dining room, without a separating door. A feature of the type B flat is the use of a pair of communicating doors from the bedroom to the living/dining room. This is particularly useful if a partner is bedfast, as with the doors open the invalid is not isolated.

With reference to the means of escape in case of fire, it should be noted that this scheme is designed for smoke containment, with doors across corridors at strategic positions.

Fig. 51 Main entrance

Fig. 52 Elevation overlooking Oxford Street

CASE STUDIES

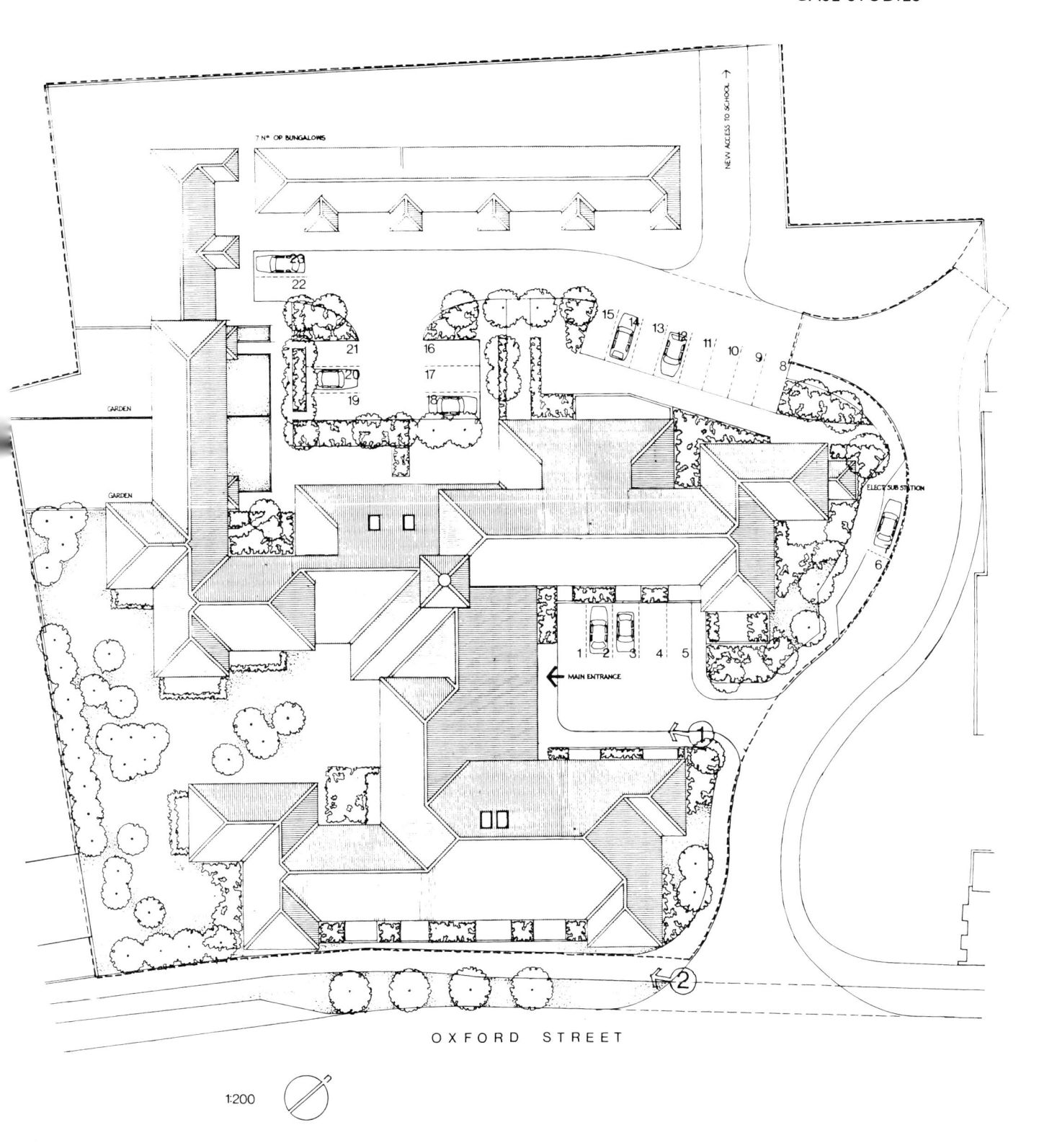

Plan 15   Site plan

CASE STUDIES

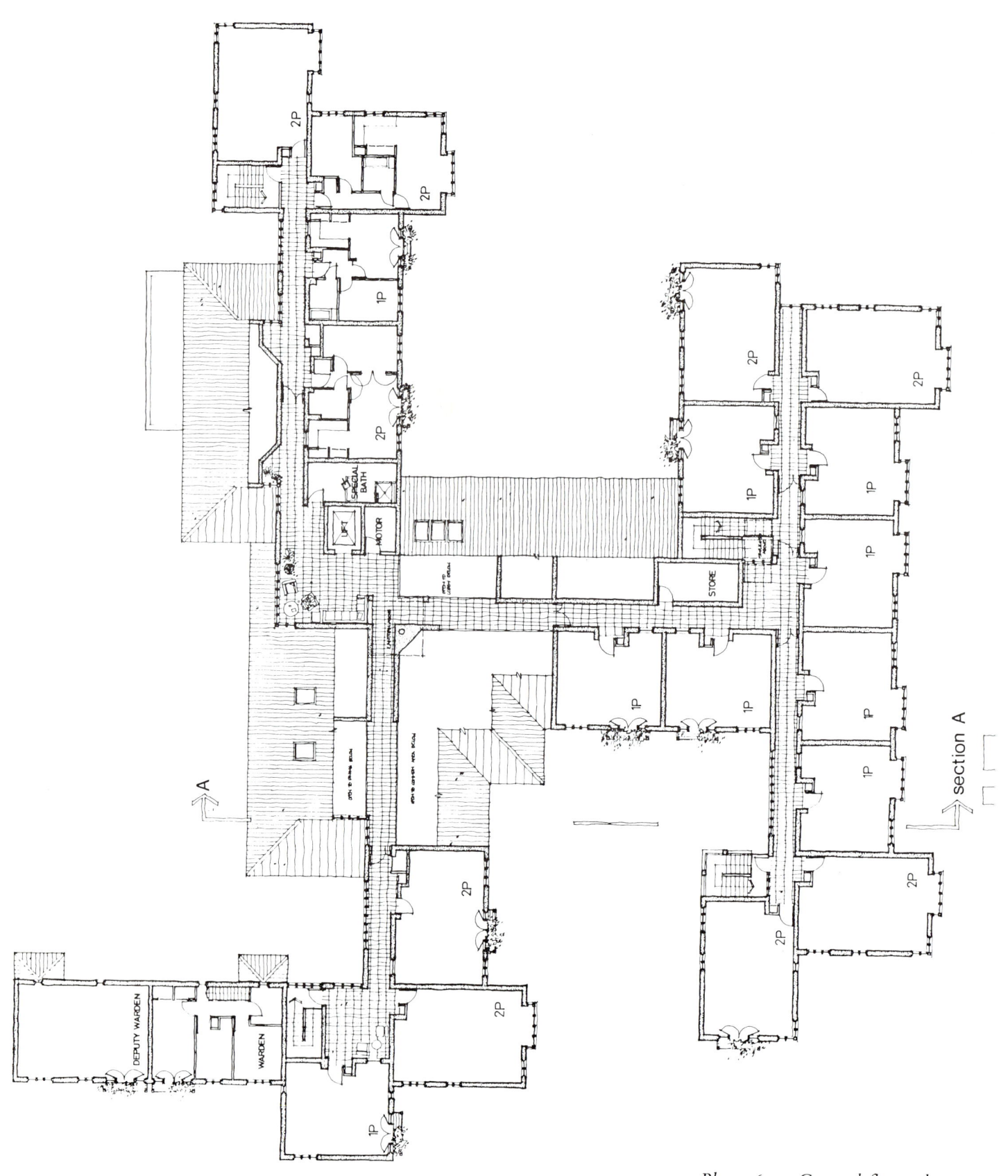

Plan 16   Ground floor plan

CASE STUDIES

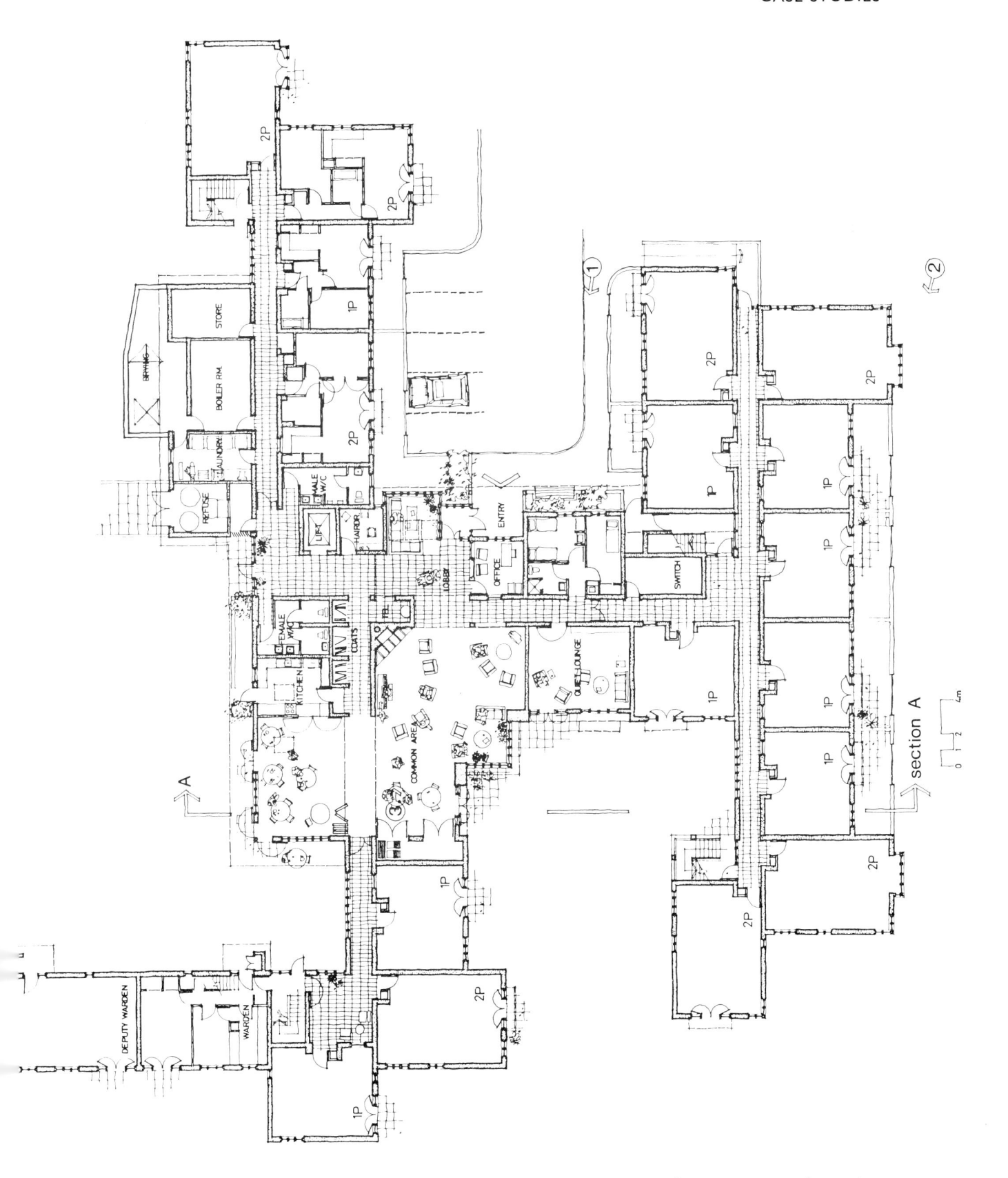

Plan 17   First floor plan

CASE STUDIES

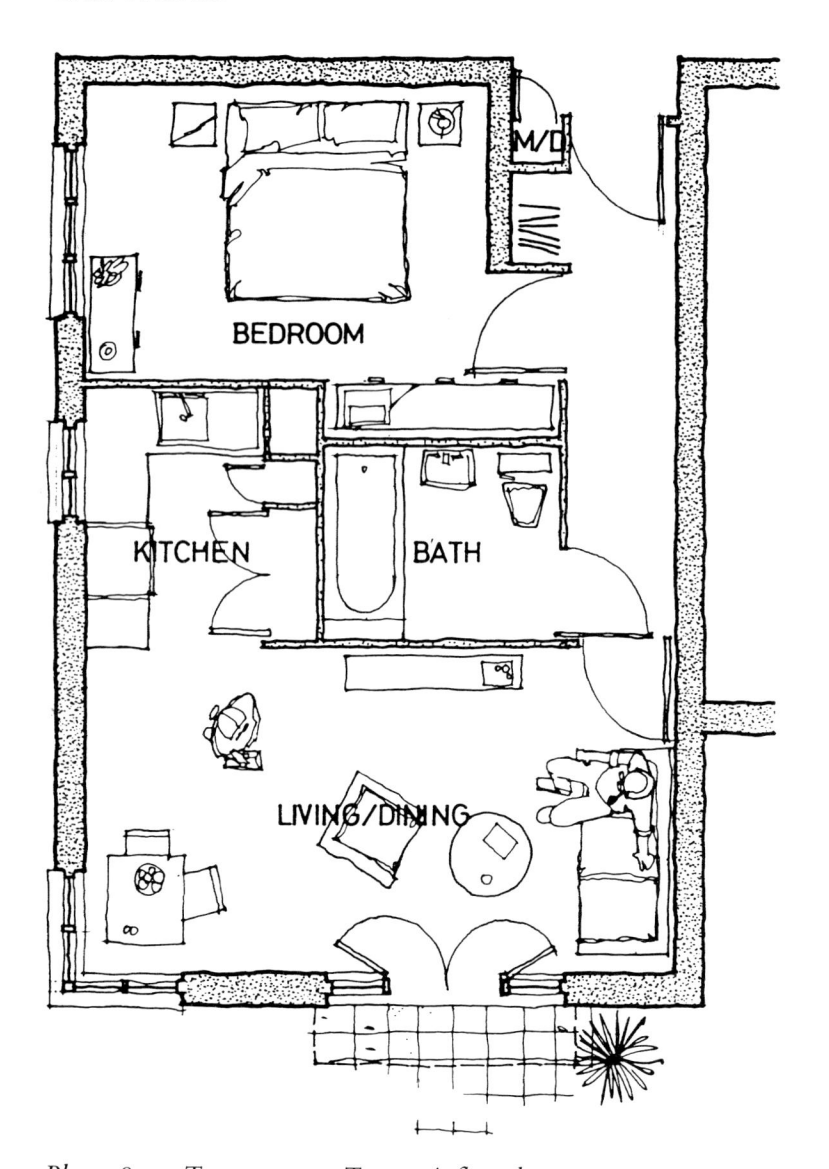

Plan 18 Two person: Type 2A flat plan

CASE STUDIES

Plan 19   Two person: Type 2B flat plan

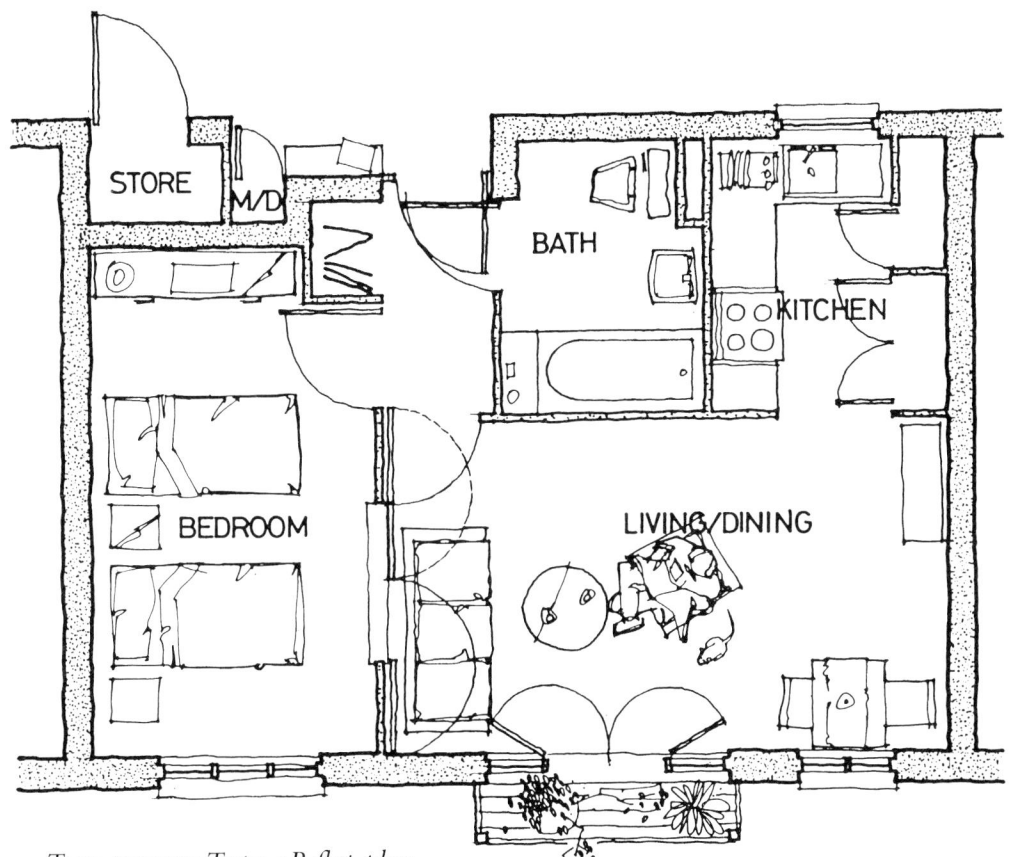

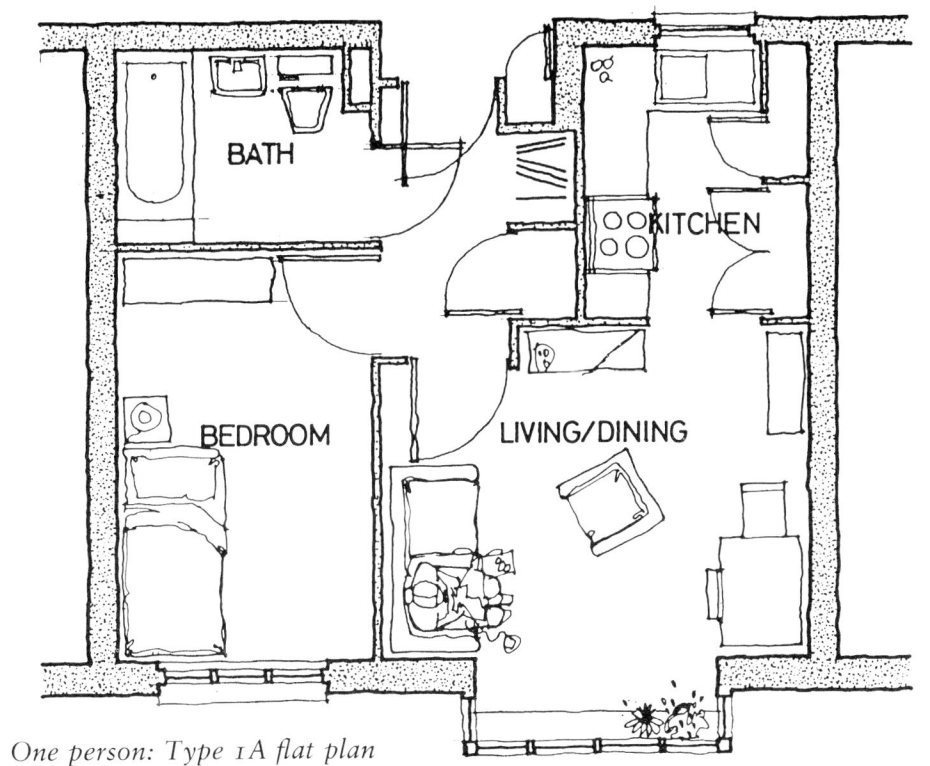

Plan 20   One person: Type 1A flat plan

123

CASE STUDIES

Category 2½: Abbeyfield housing at Hayes, Middlesex

Architects: Phippen Randall and Parkes

Client: The Abbeyfield (Uxbridge) Society Ltd.

The site, off Marshall Drive, Hayes, is in a relatively quiet position behind buildings fronting the Uxbridge Road, in a residential area close to shops and other facilities.

The present scheme was commissioned in 1978 following a proposal in 1977 to develop part of the site with an Abbeyfield house and the remainder as housing. When the housing scheme proved not to be viable the whole of the site was offered to Abbeyfield to develop with three Abbeyfield houses.

The 'Abbeyfield' principle is to create a family house for those lonely elderly people who would otherwise have to seek help from the local authority in 'sheltered flats' or an old people's home. It is seen by the Abbeyfield Society as a way in which privacy, independence and a measure of self-reliance can be preserved in a supportive atmosphere. To this end the houses are kept small, with no more than 8–10 residents, and there is a resident housekeeper to assist with preparation of the two main daily meals.

The development comprises three Abbeyfield Houses. Two houses are conventional Abbeyfield units and the third house was to have incorporated some extra-care provision. However, as the scheme developed, the need for extra-care provision was reviewed and it was decided that the third house should have the same accommodation as the other two but with provision for a lift installation at some future date.

Each of the houses has ten bedsitting rooms, a short-stay bedroom, ancillary facilities and a housekeeper's flat, in a two-storey wing with east/west orientation. The living rooms are in a single-storey wing in each house, with a south orientation, and look out over landscaped areas.

The bedsitting rooms have a built-in sink unit and a built-in wardrobe within the room. Each room will be furnished with the resident's own furniture. A small worktop with space for kettle and toaster is provided so that residents can prepare their own light meals in their room. Each bedsitting room has a view out to gardens or to an area of activity. The floor area of the bedsitting room is 17.8 m² (191.5 sq ft).

The circulation spaces are generous within each house and are naturally lit wherever possible. The living and dining room which opens off the entrance hall is the focal point of each house. The room is organised with a sitting space at the southern end and has a brick fireplace. A small paved terrace opens off the room for sitting out on fine days. An open screen separates the dining area from the sitting space and the ceiling line follows the roof line with exposed laminated timber beams to unite the whole space.

The success of these houses depends upon the residents being compatible as there is little opportunity for anyone to enjoy much privacy. Bathrooms, kitchen and dining facilities are all shared. In terms of the Heumann and Boldy scale continuum, the Abbeyfield houses are service-rich but privacy-poor. However, the small scale of these developments avoids the institutional nature of other schemes.

Fig. 53   *Entrance to House 1.*
(Photo: Crispin Boyle)

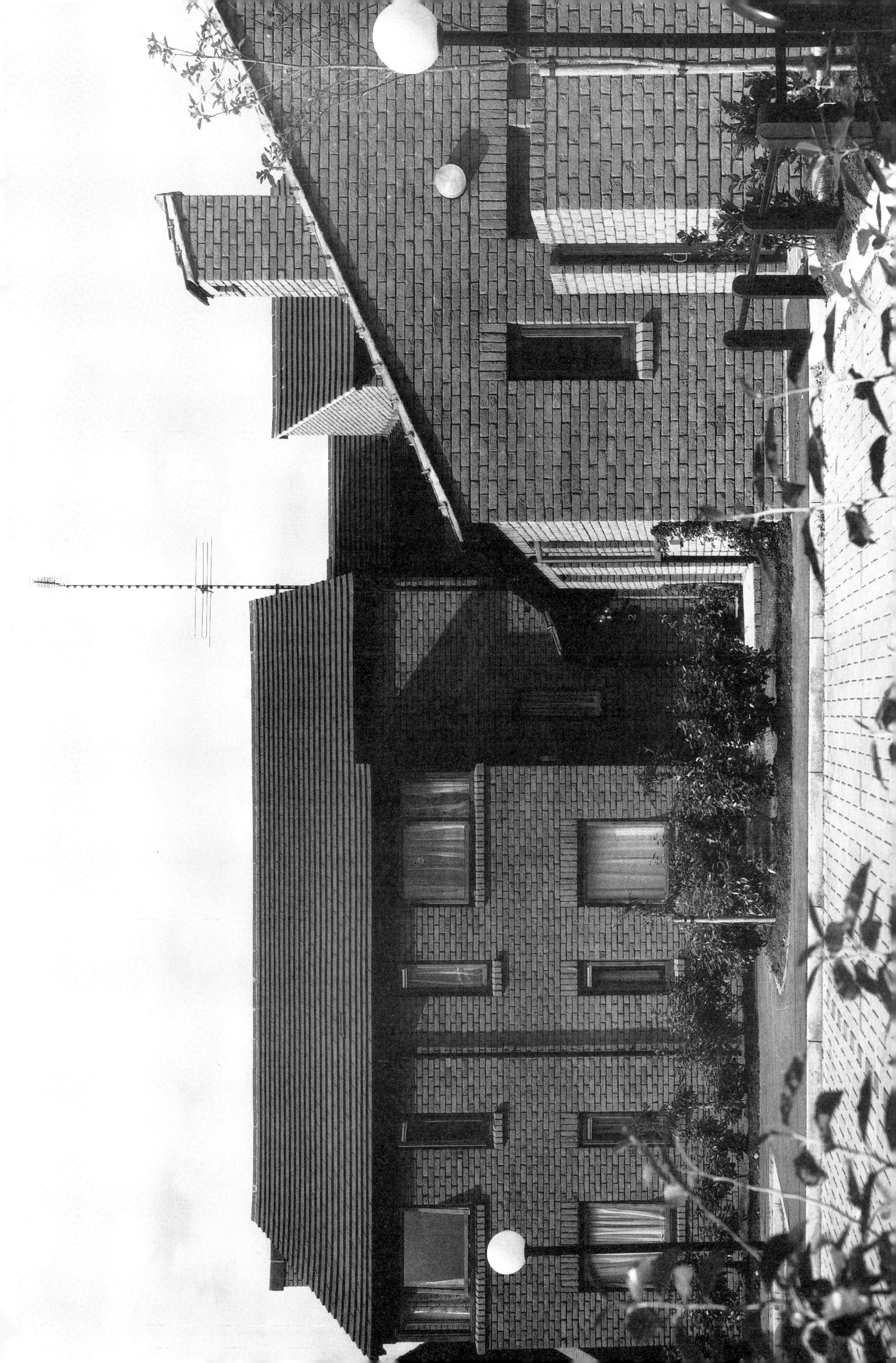

Existing house

Plan 21 Ground floor and site plan

N

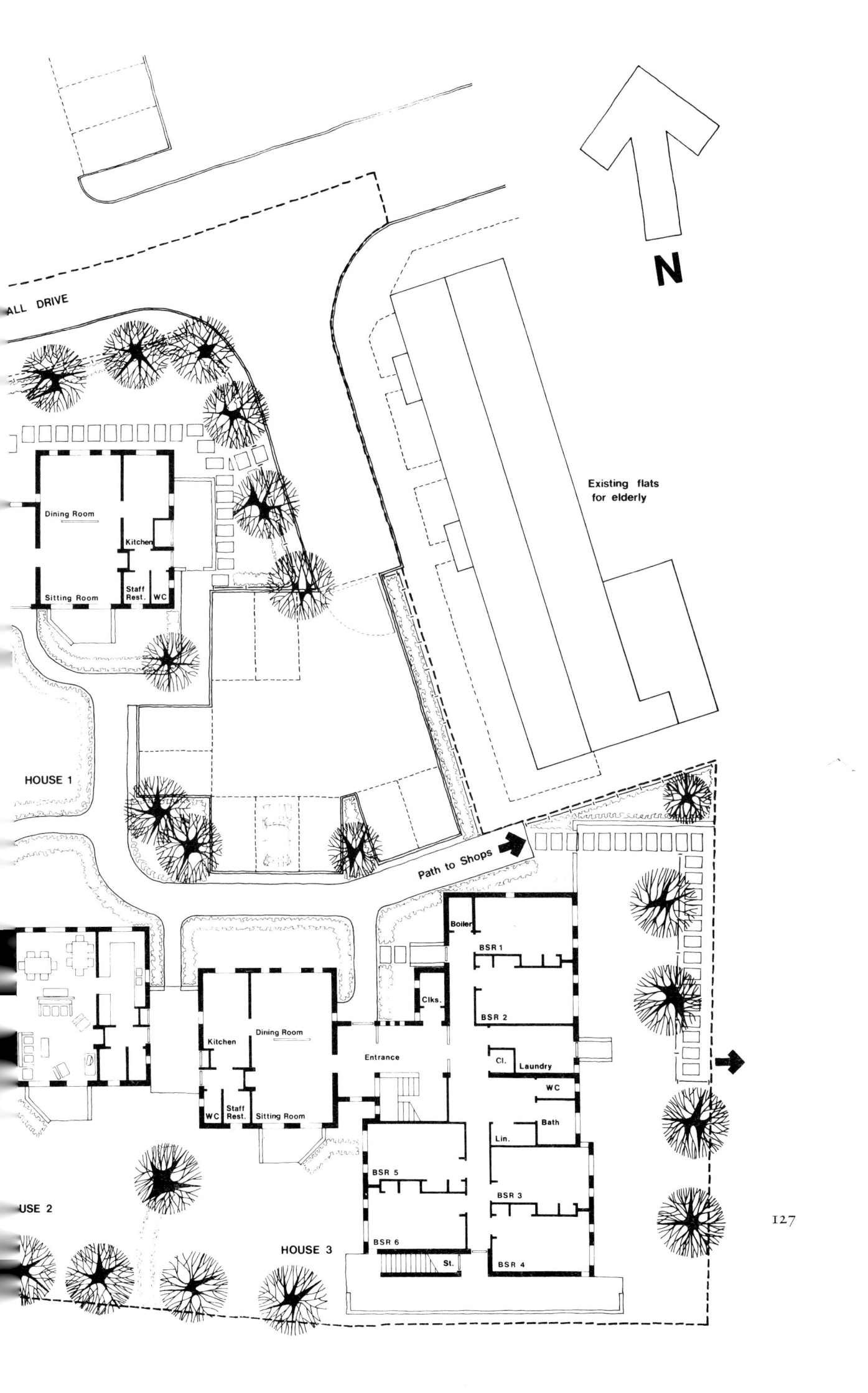

ALL DRIVE

HOUSE 1

Dining Room

Kitchen

Sitting Room

Staff Rest.

WC

Existing flats for elderly

Path to Shops

HOUSE 2

Kitchen

Dining Room

WC

Staff Rest.

Sitting Room

Entrance

Boiler

BSR 1

Clks.

BSR 2

Cl.

Laundry

WC

Bath

Lin.

BSR 5

BSR 3

BSR 6

St.

BSR 4

HOUSE 3

127

CASE STUDIES

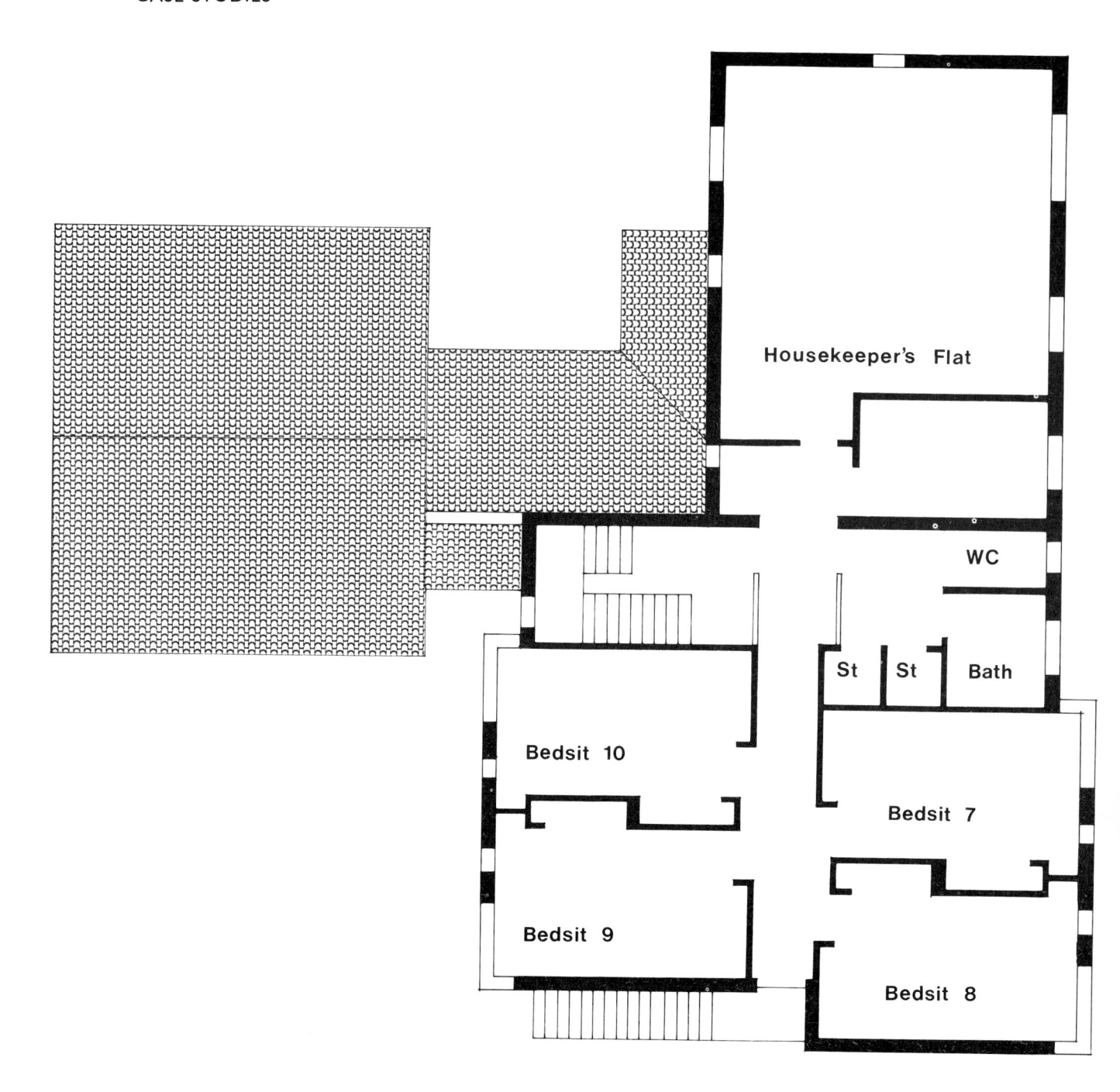

Plan 22   First floor: House 3

128

CASE STUDIES

Fig. 54 *View of House 2 with the car park in the foreground.* (Photo: Crispin Boyle)

CASE STUDIES

Categories 1, 2 and 2½: Old people's home at Almere, Netherlands

Architect: Herman Hertzberger
Client: Nederlandse Centrale voor Huisvesting van Bejaarden

The building is located near to the centre of Almere-Haven, a new town by a lake east of Amsterdam. The design was developed to house old people as a community: the accommodation provides for different degrees of independence, with bed-sit flats close to the centre of the main block and two-person, separate bedroom flats in a wing folding away from the core. Courtyard apartments for the more independent elderly are located to the south of the main building as an independent block. Active and frail elderly are all sheltered in the one complex.

The community nature of the development is reinforced by the provision of ample common space for dining and sitting, and a kitchen providing a restaurant service, with meals delivered to the flats if required or taken in the dining room. The circulation routes afford opportunities for residents to 'personalise' spaces. Recessed entrance doors adjacent to access hatches for delivery of meals or general household deliveries, wide window shelves, and the widening of corridors at strategic positions, provide spaces for tenants to furnish with plants and pictures. This opportunity to decorate the circulation space has been enthusiastically taken up.

Three types of dwellings are provided in the scheme:

1. One-person flats with a floor area of 23.33 m² (251 sq ft)

2. Two-person flats with a floor area of 47.68 m² (513 sq ft)

3. Two-person apartments with a floor area of 65.6 m² (705 sq ft)

The one-person flats comprise a bedsitting room en suite with a small kitchen and a shower/lavatory off the kitchen area. These small units are light and airy and within a limited floor space remarkably spacious and easy to furnish. For the frail elderly they offer many advantages. First, there are only two doors to negotiate, the entrance door and the shower room door. Secondly, within their own domain the residents may ignore the rest of the community by shutting the front door and curtaining the kitchen window on to the corridor, or, by opening the top half of the front door, designed like a stable door, greet passers-by and remain in touch. All the flats above ground level are provided with an external balcony for sitting out.

The two-person flats are also planned with the kitchen en suite with the living/dining room. Here again the kitchen has a window on to the corridor enabling the resident to remain in touch with passers-by. The bedroom has a sliding screen separating the sleeping space from the living area. For the reasons set out before this can be very beneficial. For ease of access to the shower/lavatory, there are doorways from the bedroom and the lobby. As with the one-person flats balconies are provided on upper floors.

The two-person apartments for the active and more affluent elderly have a kitchen/dining room separate from the living space and a study/dressing room off the bedroom.

The building is probably the most community-conscious development for the elderly in Europe to date. The scale of development is greater than is usual in the UK and the common facilities provided, which include not only the restaurant but a private resting place or chapel at roof level for the deceased, are rich in services not found in other schemes. However, the very success of the complex as a community calls into question the relationship of the residents with the neighbourhood. Practically all the residents' needs are catered for within the building and there is little motivation to participate in local affairs.

CASE STUDIES

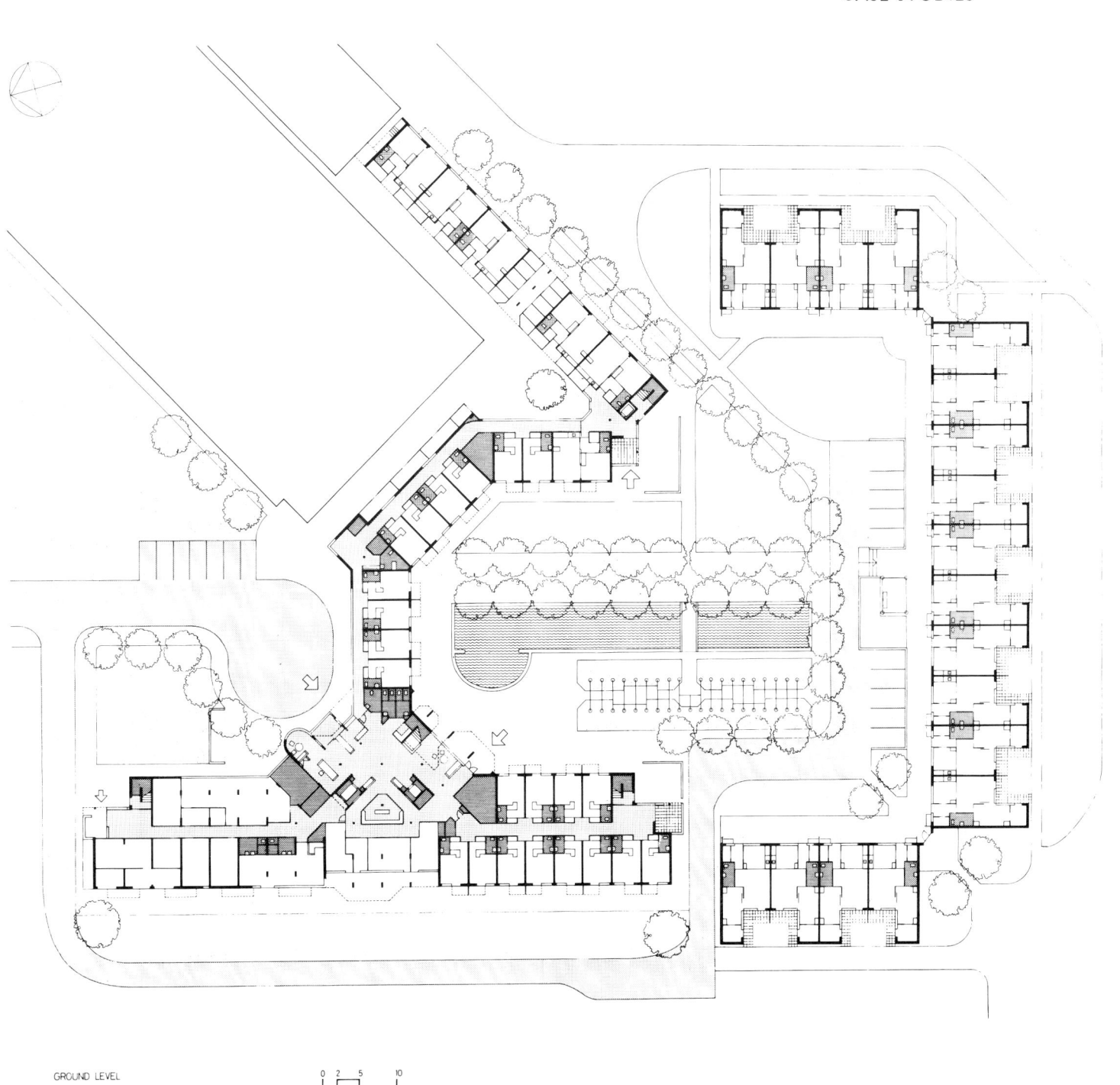

GROUND LEVEL

Plan 23   Ground floor plan

CASE STUDIES

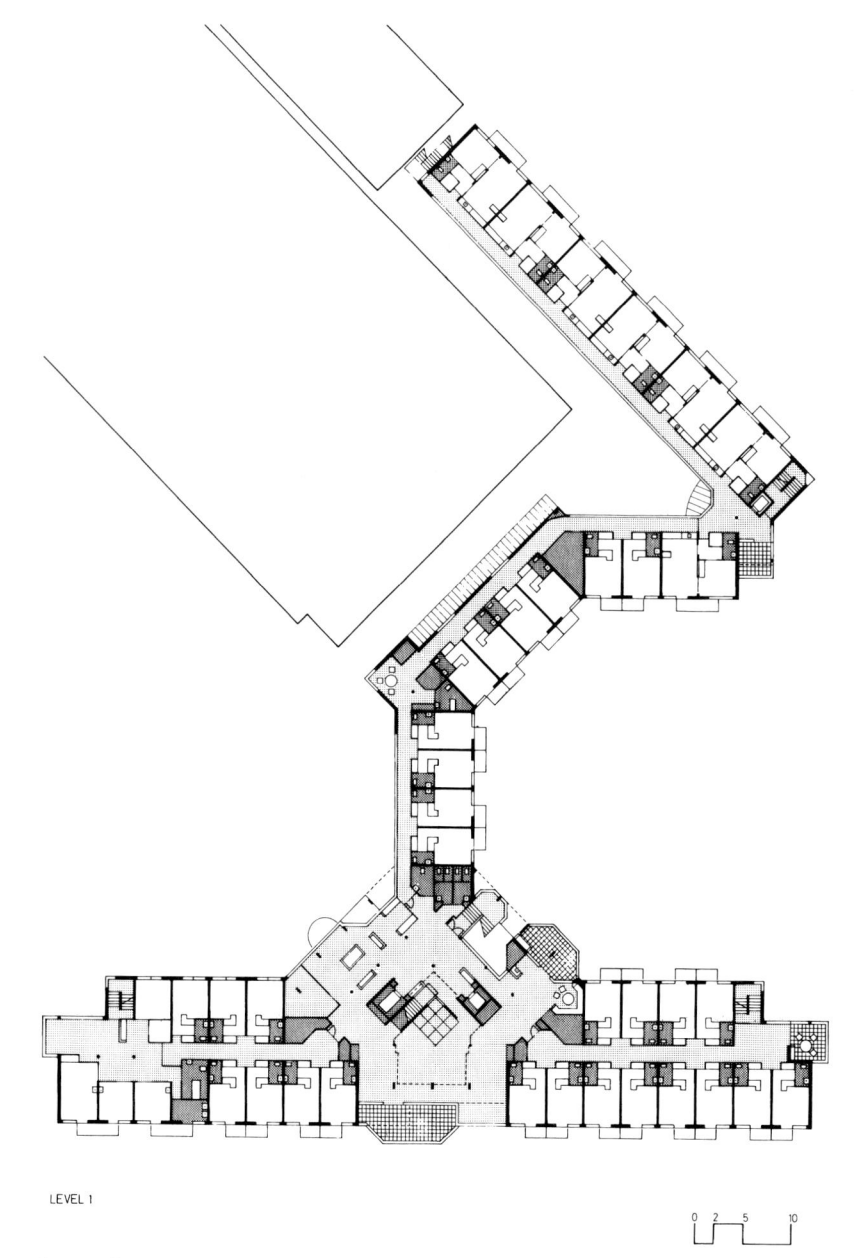

Plan 24   First floor plan

132

CASE STUDIES

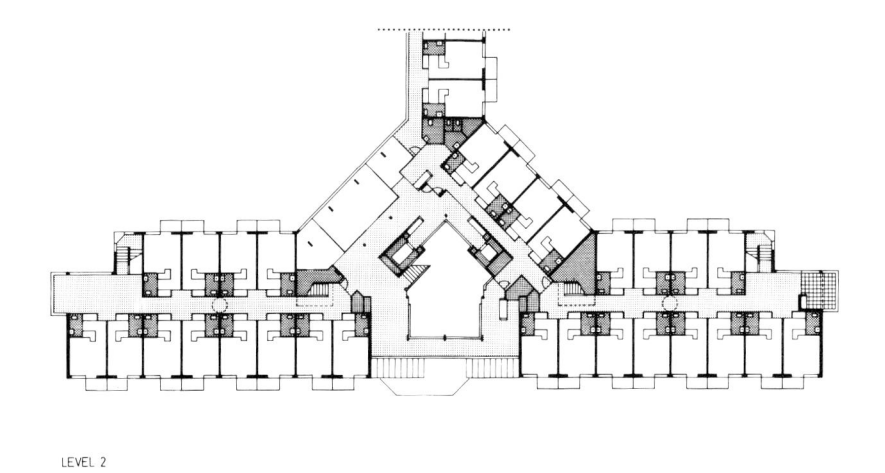

Plan 25   Second floor plan

Plan 26   Third floor plan

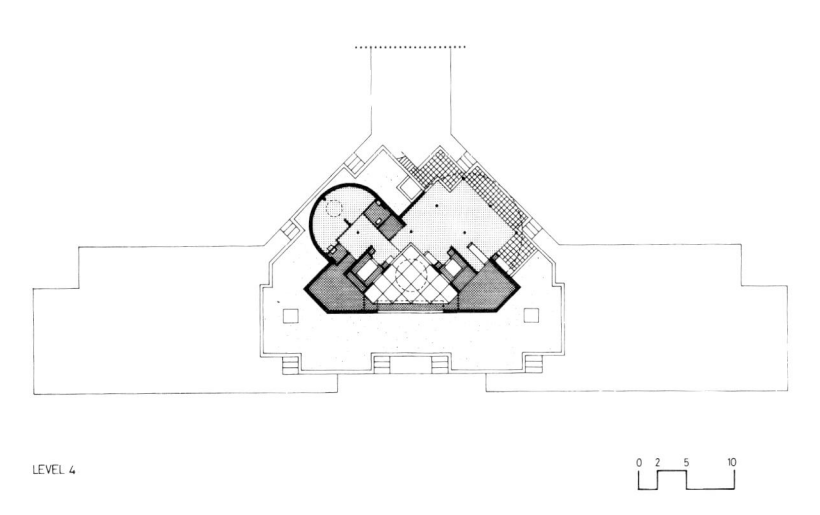

Plan 27   Fourth floor plan

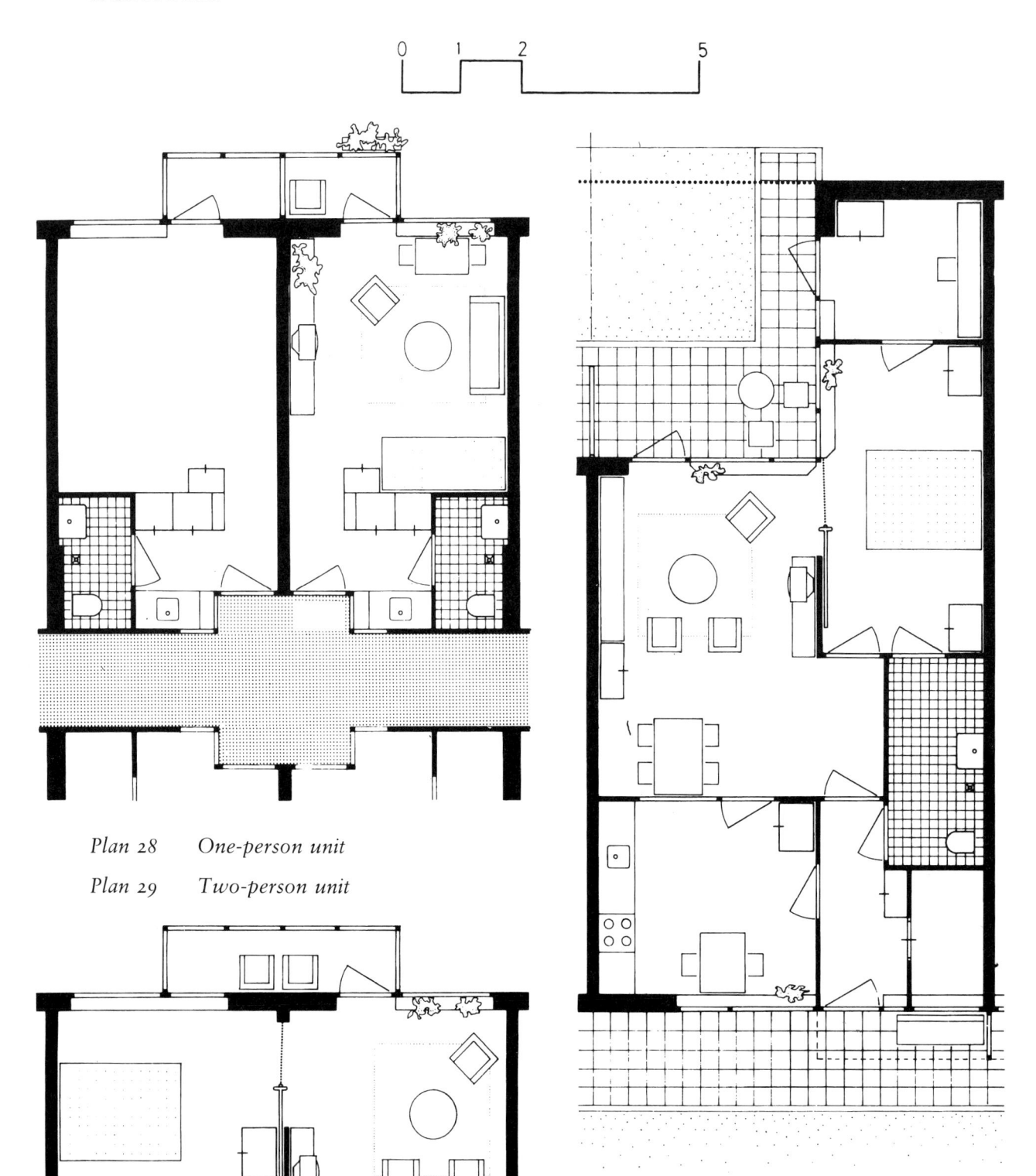

CASE STUDIES

Plan 28   One-person unit

Plan 29   Two-person unit

Plan 30   Three-person apartment

Fig. 55 Overall view with the three-person apartments in the foreground. (Photo: Martin Charles)

Fig. 56 The main entrance and car park. (Photo: Martin Charles)

Fig. 57 The residents' enclosed garden which features water, a bridge and a pergola, with seats by the waterside. (Photo: Martin Charles)

APPENDIX A: DESIGN CHECKLIST

1.00 The site and layout

1.01 Is the site within 0.4 km (0.25 miles) of shopping and leisure facilities, with a pedestrian route safe from traffic and free from steep gradients?

1.02 Is the site in a neighbourhood compatible with sheltered housing?

1.03 Will the design integrate easily with the adjoining development?

1.04 Will the proposed dwellings have an interesting outlook and enjoy some sunshine throughout the year?

1.05 Has the landscape design made provision for sheltered sitting-out space and opportunities for gardening by the elderly?

1.06 Is the pedestrian and vehicular access satisfactory for residents, visitors and large vehicles, for instance refuse collectors?

1.07 Is there provision for expansion, or reduction, of car parking space?

1.08 Will the site be secure from vandalism?

2.00 Access and circulation

2.01 Is the access from the highway well illuminated?

2.02 Is there a level access and flush threshold at the entrance?

2.03 Has provision been made to protect entrance doors from weather?

2.04 In flat developments is the foyer inviting and a suitable location for some seating?

2.05 Is the warden's office near the entrance?

2.06 Are all doorways set in a minimum 900 mm (36 in) structural opening?

2.07 Are corridors wide enough for passing (minimum 1200 mm/48 in)?

2.08 Do staircases provide an easy climb with handrails to both sides (a rise of 167 mm (6.6 in) and going of 290 mm (11.4 in) is recommended)?

2.09 Are all floor surfaces non-slip?

2.10 Will the passenger lift accommodate a wheelchair and attendant?

2.11 Has fire-fighting equipment been recessed so as not to impede progress along corridors?

2.12 Has a handrail been provided in corridors for the frail elderly?

2.13 Has a delivery hatch or shelf been provided for each dwelling?

3.00 Dwellings

3.01 Are flats handed to prevent living rooms abutting bedrooms of adjoining flats?

APPENDIX A: DESIGN CHECKLIST

3.02 Has provision been made in lobbies for the storage of hats and coats?

3.03 Are the room sizes and shapes convenient for the layout of furniture and the residents' mobility?

3.04 Will the layout permit easy access to windows?

3.05 Are window sills low enough to permit viewing out when sitting?

3.06 Are the opening lights easily accessible and safe for the elderly leaning out to reach the opening and closing gear?

3.07 Will the bedroom layout permit the bed to stand away from the wall for ease of bedmaking?

3.08 Does the bathroom door open out and can the lock be operated from the outside in an emergency?

3.09 Is the bathroom equipped with mobility aids or suitable fixing points for future aids?

3.10 Is the bathroom equipped with a medicine cabinet (not over wash basin unless recessed), a towel rail, robe hook and simple toilet roll holder?

3.11 For the frail elderly, is the bath no larger than 1550 mm (51 in)?

3.12 Are the taps easily manipulated by arthritic fingers?

3.13 Is the bathroom floor non-slip?

3.14 Is there space in the kitchen of two-person dwellings for casual meals to be taken?

3.15 Is there 1.7 m³ (60 cu ft) of storage space, including the refrigerator, in the kitchen?

3.16 Does the kitchen layout provide worktop space either side of the cooker?

3.17 Is a fire blanket provided in the kitchen by the latch side of the kitchen door?

3.18 Is general, linen and broom cupboard storage provided?

3.19 Are stopcocks, main switches and circuit-breaker fuse-boxes in convenient and well-lit positions for the elderly to operate and are meters in a position where they can be read from the outside, or alternatively without having to enter an inhabited room?

3.20 Are electrical sockets in dwellings provided in sensible positions relative to possible furniture layouts, and to the following minimum standards?
   kitchen   4
   living room   4
   bedroom   2
   bedsitting room 5

3.21 Are the emergency alarm controls positioned conveniently in relation to furniture and fittings in bedrooms, bathrooms and living rooms?

3.22 Is there provision for a communal TV aerial and is the dwelling TV aerial socket conveniently situated for daytime TV viewing?

4.00 Warden's dwelling

4.01 Is the warden's dwelling integral to or adjoining the main building and near to the warden's office?

4.02 Is there private access from the public highway for the warden?

4.03 Is there a private garden for the warden?

4.04 Can the warden view the main entrance and car park from a kitchen or living room window?

5.00 Communal facilities

5.01 Is the common room planned close to the entrance foyer and is it suitable for formal and informal functions?

5.02 Are the following provided convenient to the common room:
(a) pantry or kitchen
(b) at least one WC suitable for wheelchair use
(c) space for hats and coats
(d) storage for chairs and board games?

5.03 Is the warden's office off the entrance foyer and large enough to hold a desk, filing cabinet and two chairs, and can the entrance be viewed from the office?

5.04 Where hairdressing or hobbies rooms are planned, has provision been made for suitable sink units?

5.05 Are the following provided in the laundry:
(a) a sink
(b) one washing machine
(c) one tumble dryer
(d) space for spin dryer
(e) a table or bench for folding clothes
(f) storage for cleaning materials and ironing board?

5.06 Is the laundry floor non-slip and can it be washed down to a floor gulley?

5.07 Is there a guest room with lobby access?

5.08 Is there a shower/WC and wash basin off the guest room lobby for use by residents not able to use a bath?

5.09 Is the shower room floor non-slip?

5.10 In public housing, has provision been made for a public telephone?

5.11 Where central refuse collection points are provided, has access via a well-ventilated lobby been provided?

5.12 Have all elements generating noise, for instance lift, laundry, boiler room, been isolated from dwellings?

APPENDIX B: LIST OF ORGANISATIONS

The following organisations provide information and advice on design for the elderly:

1. United Kingdom

Abbeyfield Housing Association, 186–192 Darkes Lane, Potters Bar, Herts. EN6 1AB

Age Concern England (National Old People's Welfare Council), Bernard Sunley House, Pitcairn Road, Mitcham CR4 3LL

Anchor Housing Association, Oxenford House, 13–15 Magdalen Street, Oxford OX1 3BP

Centre on the Environment for the Handicapped, 35 Great Smith Street, London SW1P 3BJ

Department of the Environment, 2 Marsham Street, London SW1P 3EB

Habinteg Housing Association, 10 Nottingham Place, London W1M 3FL

Hanover Housing Association, 145A Merton Road, South Wimbledon, SW19 1ED

House Builders' Federation, 82 New Cavendish Street, London W1M 8AD

National Federation of Housing Associations, 175 Gray's Inn Road, London WC1X 8UP

National Housing and Town Planning Council, 14 Old Street, London EC1V 9AB

APPENDIX B: LIST OF ORGANISATIONS

2. United States of America

National Alliance of Senior Citizens
2525 Wilson Boulevard
Arlington, Virginia 22201
(703) 241-1533
C. C. Clinkscales III, National Director

National Association of State Units on Aging
600 Maryland Avenue SW Suite 208
Washington, DC 20024
(202) 484-7182
Daniel A. Quirk, Executive Director

National Caucus and Center on Black Aged
1424 K Street NW Suite 500
Washington, DC 20005
(202) 637-8400
Samuel Simmons, President

National Council on the Aging
600 Maryland Avenue SW
West Wing 100
Washington, DC 20024
(202) 479-1200
Jack Ossofsky, Executive Director

National Institute on Senior Housing
c/o National Council on the Aging
600 Maryland Avenue NW
West Wing 100
Washington, DC 20024
(202) 479-1200
Larry C. Faulhaber, Executive Officer

National Voluntary Organization for Independent Living for the Aging
600 Maryland Avenue SW West Wing 100
Washington, DC 20024
(202) 479-1200
George Thomas Beal, Director

North American Association of Jewish Homes & Housing for the Aging
2525 Centerville Road
Dallas, Texas 75228
(214) 327-4503
Dr. Herbert Shore, Executive Vice President

International Association for Housing Science
PO Box 340254
Coral Gables, Florida 33134
(305) 448-3532
Dr. Oktay Ural, President

American Institute of Building Design
1412 19th Street
Sacramento, California
(916) 447-2422
Diana Darling-Lewis, Executive Director

American Institute of Architects
1735 New York Avenue NW
Washington, DC 20006
(202) 626-7300
Louis L. Marines, Jr., Executive Vice President'

National Association of Home Builders of the US
15th and M Streets NW
Washington, DC 20005
(202) 822-0200
Kent W. Colton, Executive Vice President

Department of Housing & Urban Development
Room 10184
451 7th Street NW
Washington, DC 20410
(202) 755-7218

– Elderly Housing and Special Programs
– Federal Housing Commission

BIBLIOGRAPHY

1. Books

Age is opportunity: education and older people, Midwinter, E., 1982, London, Centre for Policy on Ageing

Bricks and Mortals: design and lifestyle in old people's homes, Norman, A., 1984, London, Centre for Policy on Ageing

Communal Facilities in Sheltered Housing, Rose, E. A. and Bozeat, N. R., 1980, Farnborough, Hants., Saxon House

Designing for Ageing: Patterns for Use, Howell, S. C., 1980, Cambridge, Massachusetts and London, The MIT Press

Designing for the Disabled, Goldsmith, S., 1976, London, RIBA Publications

Gardening for the Physically Handicapped and Elderly, Chaplin, M., 1978, London, Batsford

Housing for the Aged, Rose, E. A., 1978, Farnborough, Hants., Saxon House

Housing the Aged in Western Countries, Beyer and Nierstraz, 1967, Elsevier Publishing Co.

Housing for the Elderly, Scottish Housing Handbook 5, 1980, HMSO

Housing for the Elderly: development process, Green, I. (and others), 1974, New York and London, Van Nostrand Reinhold

Housing for the Elderly: New Trends in Europe, Goldberg, L., 1981, New York and London, Garland STPM

Housing for the Elderly: Planning Policy and Formulation in Western Europe and North America, Heumann, L. and Boldy, D., 1982, London, Croom Helm/New York, St Martin's Press

Housing for the Elderly: Privacy and Independence in Environment for the Ageing, Hoglund, J. D., 1985, New York, Van Nostrand Reinhold

Housing Interiors for the Disabled and Elderly, Raschko, B. B., 1982, New York, Van Nostrand Reinhold

Independence and the elderly, Fisk, M. J., 1986, London, Croom Helm

Site Planning and Design for the Elderly: Issues, Guidelines and Alternatives, Carstens, D.Y., 1985, New York, Van Nostrand Reinhold

Sheltered housing for the elderly: policy, practice and the consumer, Butler, A., Oldman, C. and Greve, J., 1985, London, George Allen and Unwin

The Elderly in Modern Society, Tinker, A., 1984

2. Reports, studies and occasional papers

'Anchor Tenants Survey', Fennell, G., 1985, Anchor Housing Association/University of East Anglia

'Anchor Tenants moving from Sheltered Housing into Residential Care', Way, A. and Fennell, G., 1985, University of East Anglia

'Sheltered Housing for the Elderly', Butler, A., 1984, Leeds University

'Housing for sale to the elderly: 3rd report: a review of the retirement housing market and future trends', Baker, S. and Parry, M., 1986, London, Housing Research Foundation

'Gardens and Grounds for Disabled and Elderly People', proceedings of a seminar, 1981, London, Centre on Environment for the Handicapped

'Housing alternatives for the elderly', Butler, A. and Tinker, A., 1983, Centre for Applied Social Studies, University of Leeds

'The housing needs of frail elderly people', by Bessel, R. in *Residential care for the elderly: present problems and future issues*, Laming, H., 1984, London, Policy Studies Institute, pp. 32–45

INDEX

Abbeyfield Homes 29, 31
Almshouse 15f
Anchor Housing Association 19

Bathroom 51f
Battery room 77
Bedroom 49f
Bed-sit flats 60, 116
Boiler house 76

Cars 39f
   parking ratios 39
   garages 40
   ownerships 39
Circulation space 31
Cleaners' store 76
Colours, internal 82
Common rooms 28
Communal facilities 24
Corridors 28, 82f

Defensible space 26, 37
Delivery shelves 41
Disabilities 20
Dwellings 41f

Education, further 34
Electrical switchrooms 77
Emergency alarms 96f
Empty nesters 17
Entrance to flats 41f
   foyers 62f
Environment 37f
   violent 16
Extra-care units 28f, 53f

Fire-fighting 92
Frail elderly 21
   communal facilities 77ff
   definition 31
   group model 32
   hotel model 30
   schemes 55ff

Furniture layout 43ff

Garage, cars 40
Guest room 28, 68f

Handrails 82
Health 14f, 19, 34
Heating 93f
Housekeeper 20

Independence 99

James Butcher Housing Association 29

Kitchens 46ff
   worktops 47
   taps 47
   storage 47

Landscape 84ff
   elements in 90
   public and private space 86
   vehicular and pedestrian 85f
Laundry 28, 71f
Leisure 34f
Lifts 28, 96
Living room 43ff
Lightng 95
Locks 42
Luncheon clubs 66f

Meals 23
Means of escape 92
Mobility 26, 51
   aids 52f

Neighbours 37f

Orientation and aspect 43, 49, 53

Pedestrian routes 37f, 85ff
Plants, indoors 79

Refuse disposal 74f
Relatives 19
Residential homes 21

Secretary 20
Security 19, 38
   landscape for 86
   windows 43f
Senile dementia 34
Services, meals etc 23
   mechanical and electrical 92ff
   public utilities 40
Sheltered housing categories 21f
   enter and exit, reasons for 19f
Shower 53, 68, 70
Site area 38f
   environment 34ff
   facilities 34
   location 34ff
   topography 37
Smoke dispersal 79

Tank room 77
Taps 47, 51f
Telephone 98
   kiosk 28, 74
Television 43
   aerials 98

Variables of
   privacy 24
   scale 24f
   service 21ff
Ventilation 96

Warden, definition of 18
   dwellings 28, 60f
   office 71
   service 23
Warwickshire County Council 29
Water supply 94
WCs, communal 68
Windows 43